Own Your BS

The No-Nonsense guide to your female Head Talk

Bree Stedman

Own Your BS: The No-Nonsense guide to your female Head Talk

This edition published 2019

ISBN: 978-0-9876426-7-7

Contents

Introduction

The best thing a woman can have is her shit together

- unknown

Since 2005, I've had the privilege of working with hundreds of women.

I've been honoured to be able to share in many success stories and to witness confidence blooming and lives being transformed.

I've also been the confidante, the shoulder to lean on, the teacher and the healer. I've seen behind the masks and it's troubling that in 2017 so many women are still lost behind their thoughts, stories and fears.

While working closely with women, I've seen time and time again the number of masks that ALL women wear. (Believe me, we've all got something going on; some just hide it better than others!)

"Life is so great. I'm so happy and content with my role as a mum, wife, professional woman," hides pain, hurt or anxiety.

"I enjoy life, it's all good – I couldn't ask for anything more," hides uncertainty, unworthiness, guilt and doubt.

"I'm good – you know, busy, but good," hides discontentment, dissatisfaction and disappointment.

"Yeah, they are good kids," hides "I have no idea what I'm doing, I need help, but I don't know how to ask."

Calmly answering the phone, "Hello, how can I help you?" even though you've just had an argument with a loved one and all you want to do is scream.

Keeping quiet in a room full of 'they've got it together' women, because you know if you start speaking you'll burst into tears from the sheer exhaustion you are feeling – mentally and physically.

I've witnessed how the BS (to be clear, I mean bullshit!) head talk keeps women stuck in a space that feels useless; feeling like there are no options left, no way out.

I've seen the torment in eyes as BS talk threatens to destroy what confidence a woman might have left, those stories of the past haunting her current reality, bringing her down.

I've seen too many plastered-on smiles, fake conversations and forced efforts of happiness.

These first hand, personal experiences led me firstly to making peace and owning my own BS, and secondly, writing this book.

In 2012, I 'put my own oxygen mask on' and dealt with the BS sabotaging my happiness and success, which I will share with you over the course of this book.

In 2013, I started working with women on an emotional level to help them do the same. This book is an extension of my work, written in the hope you find the power to own your BS, to create space and separation from the BS that is literally preventing you from creating and living your best life.

Doesn't that sound nice?

I have a hidden agenda. There's a bigger reason behind why I wrote *Own Your BS*.

I read a number of books, attended a number of courses that simply promote 'positive thinking', mindset or 'affirmations' to help women create some clarity around all those thoughts they have. None of it works. Not long term. None of them explain WHY the BS is there in the first place.

I'm passionate about breaking cycles; helping women feel and know they do have a choice, that power does lie within them.

In particular, I'm driven to help mothers help the people they influence the most, children.

This is close to my heart as I have two children, with individual needs, who test me every day. They've pushed me to my limits on more occasions than I can recall. But they deserve to have a mumma who can help them, really help them when emotional BS comes their way.

They show me insight into how many children in our world truly struggle to know their place and deal with their emotions in a healthy and positive manner. The stories I hear of children being diagnosed with depression, anxiety and panic attacks frightens me!

These kids are struggling, because unfortunately for many of them, their mumma is struggling and so are mumma's mumma, mumma's friend and mumma's sister. The women in our children's lives are doing their best to hide their struggles, be strong, confident and enough. Unfortunately, our children see through the façade and they feel the impact of our struggles.

I say this from experience. In the past when I felt I was losing the plot, all day, every day and even now when we've just had 'one of those moments', I know the less calm and capable I feel, the less calm and centred the kids are.

My BIG desire is to help women across our world put their oxygen masks on in a way that not only empowers themselves but gives their children, our next generation, the tools and strategies of Emotional Confidence™ – the ability to work through emotions with personal power, ownership and action.

Here are some interesting facts to get us started:

(from Headspace.org, Australian Bureau of Statistics and Anxiety & Depression Association of America)

- Studies on physical female brains only commenced in the 1990s. Prior to this, all information collected regarding emotional blocks, behaviours and healing, was identified as a result of either studies done on male brains, or studies done on baby male castrated mice. Yes, this includes medications specifically developed for females! The reason for this predominantly lies in the complexity of our hormones as a constantly changing hormonal state, which means testing is more challenging.
- 1 in 3 women admit to struggling with anxiety, stress, overwhelm and feelings of unworthiness.
- Women are twice as likely to be diagnosed with anxiety and panic attacks.
- Depression is more prevalent in women, as is PTSD (Post Traumatic Stress Disorder).
- Postnatal depression is on the rise. It is believed high levels of stress (and specifically the production of the stress hormone cortisol) contributes to this.
- Anxiety affects 1 in 8 children and is more common in children with depression, eating disorders and ADHD (Attention Deficit Hyperactivity Disorder).
- Globally, 17 million children are prescribed medications including anti-depressants, stimulants and other psychotropic (mind altering) medications every year.
- In the US, children 5 and under are the fastest growing segment of the non-adult population prescribed with antidepressants.

Now I don't know about you, but those statistics scare the heck out of me, encouraging me to follow this path in the first place.

Personal disclosure: I do believe that medication is sometimes required to help stabilise a person's emotional state; at times it is necessary as an intervention of sorts. Both my children use medication to help them with the effects of ADHD and I've worked with many women who use medication at times to elevate them out of situations of emotional distress. Having said that, I do feel that what is lacking in our approach to working with emotional blocks (head talk and emotional meltdowns/moments) is the coping strategies, information and processes to help a person live life, in all its ups and downs, with Emotional Confidence™.

I believe medication by itself and standard therapy practices for women do not take into consideration the Female Factor. They do not seem to help long term.

The goal of this book is to give you insight and strategies to help yourself claim your power over the emotional BS you keep getting caught up in, so you can teach those people nearest to you, especially children in your life, these coping strategies.

What makes this book different from other self-help books on the shelf?

I share information about why you, as a female, differ from the way males process emotional stories. I share insight into how you can work with your Female Factor to create a life that works with the natural cycle your life is built upon. I share with you a number of case studies from women I've worked with during the past 4 years, who have transformed their lives as a result of working with their brain and personal feminine cycle.

This book is chock-a-block full of strategies and tools you can start using straight away! Activities and insightful exercises throughout each chapter will help you identify your BS, do something about it, and learn from it for the future.

What makes me qualified to write a book like this?

Me! My life experiences, my journey with this information, strategies and tools. I share my story throughout pockets in this book, however it's good for you to know now that everything in this book has been tried and tested extensively by me. After I mastered it myself, I spent the last few years teaching, helping, mentoring and encouraging other women to do the same.

Between 2006 and 2017, I mentored, educated, trained and helped hundreds of women build businesses and better understand themselves, then build inspiration and motivation from within.

I spent the best part of 2012-2013 learning what I could about the female brain, how we process emotional situations, how we heal from emotional blocks and how to uncover deeply seeded beliefs which hold negative habits in your life. I was one of the first women in the world to be trained in an exclusively 'for the female brain' process called Creatrix® through the Institute of Women International in Australia.

Since then, I've had the privilege of working with hundreds of women, spending more than 1500 hours specifically facilitating Creatrix® transformations for my clients with the Female Factor in mind.

What Causes the BS to Start in the First Place?

Numerous factors cause the BS to start and we are going to explore them in detail over the course of this book. One I'd like to explore now is women losing sight of what they really want in life. Women get caught up in a replay loop of storytelling and revisiting the past because they've lost sight of who they are and what they want for the future. They've lost direction, their sense of self, a sense of purpose and their passion to make the most of each day. Essentially, they are stuck!

Often the BS builds up slowly; it's rarely a significant moment where peace of mind is deliberately replaced with monkey mind. After years of dedicating themselves and their energies to the roles they play in life, such as being a good mum, a supportive partner, a valuable employee or a successful professional, they slowly lose sight of what they want for themselves as individuals.

So the stories start.

Regrets of what they should have done instead of what they did. Embarrassment they feel from the way they reacted to a situation. Pain of an argument or a confrontation with someone. Memories of events they pushed down because it was expected they 'just let it go'. Disappointment that life hasn't panned out the way they thought it would.

Before they know it, there are so many stories and so much noise, they live life as if in an emotional fog.

Is all this emotional fog BS? No, it's not. Some of those stories and thoughts you are telling yourself are valid. The human brain processes somewhere between 50,000 and 80,000 thoughts every single day, of which up to 80% are repeated thoughts from previous days. That means at a minimum, 40,000 thoughts you had yesterday were repeats. 40,000 redundant, expired, BS thoughts which no longer serve you or make a positive difference to your current life experience.

Of course, you are not consciously aware of what these thoughts are. Your conscious mind is only focused on stories you currently deem to be most important (which is why you possibly feel your life is flat and stuck, because consciously you're only aware of the stories which leave you feeling low, down, lost, sad etc.).

In fact, your conscious mind doesn't have the capacity to process that level of information. With less than 10% power of your brain, the conscious mind is predominantly focused on what your daily existence and experience looks like.

The job of sorting through thousands and thousands of thoughts is for your unconscious mind, also known as your subconscious mind. Your unconscious mind powers more than 80% of every day functioning. It's a powerful piece of machinery and when you know how to work with it, amazing things can happen!

- The unconscious mind preserves and runs your body.
- It stores and sorts your emotions and memories, which is key for females in particular, as your unconscious mind will store memories according to the emotions connected to the memories, as well as store information in terms of chronological order, themes of similar

nature, people, experiences and a number of other categories. This is why random information can be recalled; your unconscious mind has connected the dots between two events for you.

- The unconscious mind sees your life in pictures only. Logical order, rationalising, words, correct grammar etc. do not matter to your unconscious brain as it sees everything via pictures.

- The unconscious mind forms all your habits including physical, emotional and thinking habits. For instance, while learning how to drive, you had to be incredibly conscious about every movement you made, changing gears, using the indicators and turning the wheel – it was all very conscious at the beginning. The more you did it, the more the movements and decisions became a habit and the details of that habit now live within your unconscious mind. This is a physical habit. You also have emotional and thinking habits such as those instincts which cause you to be 'naturally' negative, cynical or look for the bad in a situation.

- The unconscious mind does not process negative words such as don't, which I will explain further in later chapters. Essentially, it means when you tell someone, or yourself, "Don't let me forget to grab bread and milk on the way home!" your mind hears only, "Forget the bread and milk." So guess what? You forget and have to go without your morning coffee and toast!

- The unconscious mind suppresses memories and emotions it believes you can't handle. The most important job of the unconscious mind is to support you, keep you safe and give you what you want, so those deep emotions holding your stories together are often suppressed until you consciously develop the strategies and strength to deal with them.

- When you consciously set yourself a goal, it's the unconscious mind working to make the goal a reality. The success of that goal comes down to how you feel and what you see about that goal.

- Lastly, the unconscious mind takes everything personally, so regardless of whether you are speaking about someone else negatively, or you say some something flippantly about yourself, your unconscious mind is going to take it as a direct insult. When you say they/he/she/them, your unconscious mind hears 'you'. When you say 'you' to someone else, your unconscious mind interprets that as 'you' personally. Be mindful of what you say about other people, as well as how you speak to yourself, because your unconscious mind is listening and its aim is to please!

Uncovering what is going on within the unconscious mind is a conscious job. It's something you are going to have to remind yourself of until it becomes a happier and more beneficial habit.

CASE STUDY: Julie – Married, Mother of 2, Part-Time Employment

When I first met Julie, she was constantly struggling with negative head chatter. She was in a habit of looking for the problem in every situation, always doubting herself and the situations in her life. She was regularly teary, anxious and wanted out. Out of her marriage, her home, her life. This habitual way of thinking was affecting the relationship she had with her husband and children. It impeded her ability to function in the moment as she was constantly focused on the past and her fear of the future. Regular thoughts Julie had at this time included, "I'm not good enough", "I need approval", "Why do I take things so personally?", "I don't deserve to be happy", "I'm fed up" and "I'm unlikeable". This emotional fog clouded her judgement about what life was actually like; all of her attention and thoughts were centred around finding information to back up the negative stories.

Nothing in Julie's life felt like it was enough, even with all the personal development, psychologist appointments, changing her diet and hours of soul searching. Julie was constantly trying to improve herself but couldn't move the cloud over her head.

Finally, it was enough. Julie had had enough of feeling like shit. She was sick and tired of her thoughts and the effect they were having on her marriage. She thought her only option was to leave her relationship, something she really didn't want to do. Ultimately, Julie came to the realisation that before walking away, she had to stop pointing the finger at situations around her and step up. Changing her mindset had to come from within her; changing her physical circumstances wasn't the answer.

Since Julie took ownership of her BS and the cyclic thinking pulling her down, she enjoys having more control and the negative story no longer controls her thinking. "I can recognise that I was focusing on all the wrong things, and can now appreciate myself more, being kinder to myself and my self-worth. Strangely enough, I can even feel my gut... When something feels right, I can trust my gut feeling – this is something I never felt before, I know what people mean now when they say 'trust your gut' – you really do just know! Most importantly, I am aware that my stories are MY choice. I know life has its ups and downs, but I have tools to use now to prompt me out of the downward spiral. And I appreciate the BLAH! days – in the past I would use these days as proof that my life was really bad, but these days now remind me that life is good. There doesn't need to be a drama or a 'situation'; there are no problems that I can't overcome"

Julie's story is a powerful example of what can happen when you really OWN your BS! No amount of outside help will create a significant shift for you until you get to a place where you are truly ready to take control, create new, stronger habits and let go of the BS that is not serving you.

That's the aim of this book: to guide you through a process that brings awareness around your BS, to give you strategies to create acknowledgement of your part in your life, and to give you actionable steps to increase your sense of power– a boost of passion and shine-a-light-on what your purpose (for now) is!

It's your wake-up guide, your kick-up-the-bum for you to uncover how much BS you are telling yourself, how to work through the nonsense with powerful strategies and how to retrain your brain to be positive, proactive and powerful.

Are you ready?

CHAPTER 1

What my BS is telling me

Freeing yourself was one thing;
claiming ownership of that freed self was another

Toni Morrison

I hate being a mum.

That thought is the realisation that saved my marriage, my children and me in 2012.

Let me back up a bit.

In 2007, I became a mother for the first time, to our son, Blair. The lead-up to having him was challenging. At 21 I was told it was unlikely we'd ever conceive. When I finally fell pregnant, after more than 3 years of trying, we were naturally ecstatic. With severe morning sickness throughout the entire pregnancy, early labours and 5 weeks of bedrest, my pregnancy was difficult. Blair made his entrance a couple of weeks early in March of 2007.

We were blessed with an incredibly well-behaved baby. He was happy and content, never cried, never fussed and was, by all observations, perfect.

After a second difficult pregnancy, his baby sister, Alivia followed in 2009. Shortly afterward, my husband, Aaron, and I made the decision to move from Central NSW, Australia to the Newcastle area, on the coast.

Around this time, I noticed a 'bad mood' coming over me more often than in previous years. I dismissed it as a combination of exhaustion and homesickness. Alivia was a dreadful sleeper, Aaron was working long hours at work and spent longer hours renovating the rundown house we'd bought and Blair was entering his most challenging years. Although we had some family in Newcastle and I was slowly meeting people, it wasn't the same as the comfort and ease of our home area.

On top of all of this, I was also re-building my independent business in direct sales while trying to keep the area I'd built in Orange functioning profitably.

Logically, it made sense I would experience a 'bad mood' from time to time.

I pushed it all down and continued to soldier on.

At the time, I believed that for me to be seen and accepted as a professional, I must never show my emotional struggles. Instead, I should be the example of what 'put together' looked like, to inspire other young mums I was working with at the time.

My 'bad mood' at home increased in intensity over the next few years. I avoided looking into it too much; instead I put all my focus into building my professional empire. I rapidly created a reputation for myself as a positive, influential leader other women could look up to. It inflated my ego and sense of belonging to be 'that woman'.

The problem was, I was out of balance. There were some serious misalignments happening within me, bubbling just under the surface, waiting to explode. And boy, did they explode.

During this time, Blair's behaviour started to really get out of hand. From the moment he could stand, he was running. As he learned to speak and think for himself, his strong, independent streak would regularly show itself. As we were still relatively new in Newcastle, I hadn't formed great support networks for babysitting, so where possible, I would take both my kids to work with me during the day. I vividly remember women telling me Alivia was welcome to accompany me (she was only 18 months at the time and easily contained in a high chair with some snacks), but Blair was not welcome. He was 'too wild' and 'out of control'.

While this cut me to the core, I laughed it and similar comments off, agreeing to my clients' terms, scheduling appointments around Blair's pre-school days so I only had Alivia with me. I did this because my professional success was the one thing I took pride in, that I got recognition and praise for. It always won over any negative situation at home. On reflection, I see I was making this choice because I was in a terrible headspace at home. My business was my saviour in many ways, and to defend Blair's behaviour was to reject business and clients. I couldn't compromise, regardless of the personal cost, or so I believed.

As my internal struggle to make peace with my role as a mum became difficult to hide, other mums and people of good intention would blame Blair's behaviour for why I was feeling as I was. It was a logical excuse. He was hard work so of course it was natural for me to feel upset, drained, fed up and over it.

What no one saw was how I behaved while we were at home. Yes, Blair was a challenge. Alivia was a challenge in her own way too. Ultimately, they were little children trying to find their way in a less-than-ideal environment.

No one saw how my 'bad mood' escalated to the point of raging, screaming lunatic. I was the ultimate crazy psycho mum. I was out of control and verbally abusive. Physically, I pushed the limits of appropriate too many times. Emotionally, I was all over the place, cycling between rage and anger, to guilt and shame, resentment, embarrassment, sad and lonely, often in tears before 8am. Aaron received multiple phone calls a day of me screaming, "I can't do this anymore!".

I hid it all.

Family and friends knew I was struggling with Blair, but had no idea how bad I was handling the situation. I hid it from everyone because I knew it was unacceptable. I felt so guilty and ashamed. I feared if I voiced my struggles out loud I'd open the door for criticism, judgement or sympathy, none of which I wanted.

I knew 'professional women' didn't behave that way. I knew should anyone find out the depths of my struggles, my children would be taken away from me. I knew if people saw the real Bree, I would be rejected by friends and support networks. I firmly held onto these beliefs which kept me trapped in a cycle of complete BS.

I attended a number of parenting courses. The pre-school arranged for Blair to be assessed and we had meetings with expert parenting coaches. These avenues of help pointed the finger squarely at Blair – he was the problem, keep doing the 'discipline' thing regardless of how exhausted you are or how much time he takes up and don't worry about your other child, your businesses or anything else. All your focus needs to be on 'dealing' with his behaviour.

That really didn't settle well, as I couldn't help but think, "How can a 4-year-old be responsible for his mumma losing the plot?"

I threw myself into any personal development course or help I could, providing it allowed me to maintain the exterior façade I desperately tried to hold in place. I didn't let anyone go too deep. I did numerous leadership programs, mindset and mindfulness courses, meditated and read affirmation books. While some of these methods would help me for a short period of time, it wouldn't be long before the Raging Bull reared her crazy head again. It didn't make any difference how many times I said the affirmation, "I am a calm and confident mum". Internally, I knew it was BS and my actions were anything but 'calm and confident'.

During one of these personal development courses, I learnt the concept of awareness, that is, becoming aware of what I was saying to myself. This is why I know, without doubt, the power of listening to the BS you tell yourself.

My inner dialogue went something like this:

"It wasn't supposed to be this hard."

"Why can't he just be a normal kid?"

"Why can't she sleep more than 2 hours?"

"Why do we have to live in this shitty house? Why did we buy it? Why can't we just be rich?"

"I'd better suck it up; it's not professional to show your emotions. Remember who you are to her!"

"Look at her, she's got it all together, I'll never be as good as her."

"No wonder she's successful, she doesn't have 2 brat kids at home."

"You are such a bitch, I can't believe he loves you."

"I hate this. I hate my life. I hate being a mum."

Once I started listening to these thoughts, becoming really clear about what I was saying, I was appalled. Who was this person? Yet, it made complete sense. No wonder I was feeling like crap all the time. Who wouldn't with that kind of nonsense running on replay? Until that time, I felt powerless, trapped in a cycle of shitty circumstances, with extremely limited options available to me. Now I knew what I was saying to myself, I felt a sense of power come over me. If I started thinking these thoughts, maybe I could stop thinking them too!

If only it was that easy! I still had a lot to learn, but at least I now had hope and something to work with!

Why is it so hard for women to stop thinking the negative, nasty stories we tell ourselves? Why couldn't I just stop thinking, "I hate my life" and instead, think, feel and believe, "I love my life"?

The answer to this question has two elements:

1. The filters every story and event run through before an emotion is assigned to it.

2. Your female brain and the head/heart connection.

The Filters

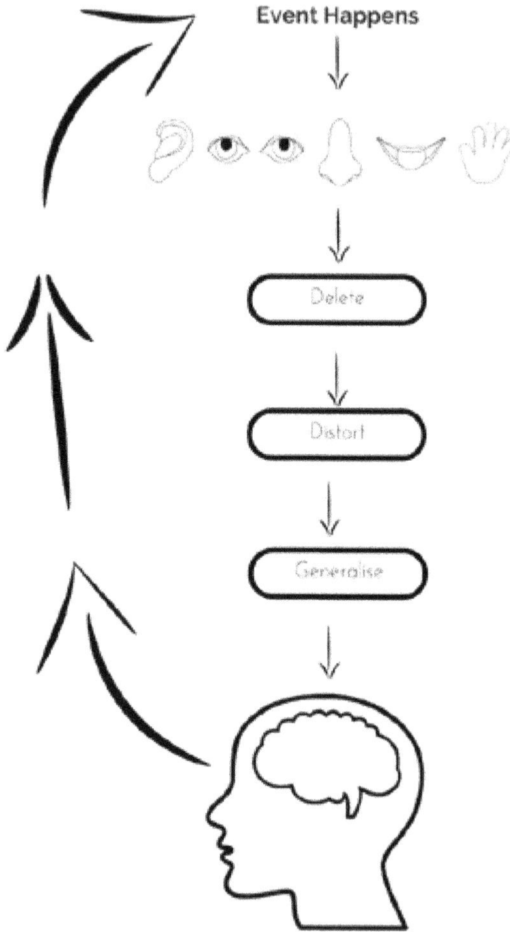

For every event you experience, your brain goes through a very rapid process of identifying, analysing and assigning a thought, emotion and reaction.

The event is processed in our brain through a series of filters. These filters reduce the amount of information processed so your conscious mind can experience the event.

Think of these filters like sunglasses. If you were wearing more than one pair of sunglasses at once, you wouldn't see much of what was really going on, would you?

There are filters that will delete, distort and generalise information so you only see what your conscious mind will allow you to see. This process is habitual, so if you have a habit of generalising a population, the current (and future) events will have this filter applied without conscious consideration.

If your inner dialogue is reflecting a negative mind space, this conscious focus is going to only see a negative outcome. Identifying the truth means sorting through the filters to see reality without the filters altering it.

The filters of your past memories and experiences, current hormone levels, mindset and mood will further distort, generalise and delete fractions of the event to create your reaction.

For example, while driving, a car pulls out in front of you. In that split second, you visually see the car and you hear the kids yelp. Your filter deletes the female passenger in the front of the car and distorts the silhouette of the male driver. It then creates a generalisation because somewhere in your childhood you heard your father say, "All old ladies are bad drivers!" then as your oestrogen levels drop, you feel anger and impatience fly up to the surface. Your road rage creates a story that the driver of the vehicle is an old lady and while 'she' continues to drive on her merry way, you are left cursing and raging in your car. This event has been assigned anger and frustration as the required emotional response and unconsciously it will be filed into your memories of bad drivers with those attached emotions.

Your brain has processed this event according to your filters, reinforcing your beliefs and providing evidence to your current mindset. What your brain doesn't see is the female passenger who was in labour while her husband, the driver, only uses his indicator for a split second before merging into your lane because he too, is caught up in his own world and situations.

Your brain filters are responsible for your perception of the world, as my filters are responsible for the way I see my world. It's important to know every person perceives every situation differently based on their filters. Rather than jumping to conclusions next time you feel yourself react negatively, question how much of what you think you saw/felt/heard is true and how much could just be misperceived.

CASE STUDY: Chantelle – Married, Pregnant Mother of 1, Vet Nurse

Chantelle felt no love for herself prior to owning her BS. She didn't set goals, have a vision or understanding of her values. She felt undeserving and unworthy, sad and lonely, despite having a wonderful husband and beautiful daughter. She kept her emotions hidden and quite guarded. She felt the need to constantly prove herself, she feared vulnerability, and brushed aside or downplayed her previous achievements and accomplishments. She would beat herself up over minor mistakes and past decisions. Without realising it, Chantelle carried a large amount of resentment, would react to bad experiences in the work place and then bottle the feelings up, further fuelling a lack of confidence and a sense of calm.

The more time she spent with her growing daughter, and as the possibility of a sibling approached, she began to crave being the best person she could be, to be the role model she deserved to be. She wanted brushed to be able to voice the love she felt for her husband, to appreciate him without feeling fearful of vulnerability and rejection. She yearned for self-love and true happiness.

Since owning her BS, Chantelle has more confidence and knows the full responsibility of who she is and what she wants. "I have absolute confidence in my decisions – I no longer hold grudges; I have created boundaries that have created space for more energy. I'm able to listen so much more, while detaching from the emotional baggage, situations and people that do not serve me. Vulnerability is exciting for me now – I speak up and I can see ahead of me a much more clearer vision. I believe the confidence in my decisions have created more confidence and direction for my daughter – our bond is amazingly strong. I have found a true appreciation and love for others that I never believed was possible."

The Female Head/Heart Connection

As a female, your brain is more emotional by nature, and to every single thought you have, whether consciously acknowledged or not, an emotion is assigned. You do this 25% more often than men. Once an emotion is assigned to an event or story, that story is harder to detach from.

What does this actually mean?

In the example of the above car incident, you've attached anger and frustration. If you were a man, you would experience that car incident and let it go without too much consideration. Because you are female, you find yourself still feeling angry and frustrated hours later. When the kids start arguing that night, you unconsciously remember the car incident, which adds another dose of anger and frustration to the kids' argument. These recent events aren't the only events fuelling your emotional reactions; you unconsciously recall a series of memories where anger and frustration were assigned, making this argument with the kids seem much bigger than it really is.

Every time you revisit those events, telling a friend about the car incident or telling your partner about the kids arguing, your brain revisits those emotions of anger and frustration, further locking in the emotional connection.

How does this happen? Between your conscious mind and unconscious mind there is a net-like area called the Reticular Activating System (RAS). The RAS is the 'go-between' for the two minds, essentially feeding whatever the conscious mind is thinking of to the unconscious mind then relaying the evidence the unconscious mind finds back to the conscious mind to support the focus.

Every story you tell yourself is anchoring in the emotions of what you've felt in the past because of the RAS. If they are positive memories, the RAS will bring your conscious focus a sense of peace, calm, love and contentment. If the memories are negative, and the emotions are draining, your RAS will bring your focus to those negative emotions – anger, frustration, guilt and stress.

With the build-up of emotional fog in your mind at present, your RAS will be feeding your unconscious with the need for evidence to support the fog. You will likely see multiple examples of times you've spoken about, or thought about the challenges in your life and each time you think about these negative stories, you make the story bigger and harder to 'get over'.

The stories end up building so much momentum and noise that the emotions almost take over, hence the emotional fog!

This is why the first strategy I'm going to share with you is going to be your golden ticket to ownership!

Now that you know how your brain assigns an emotion or reaction and why your brain keeps cycling over the same stories and events over and over again, it's time to create some space!

Until you become consciously aware of what those inner thoughts are, your power remains with your thoughts and accompanying emotions.

In my 'I'm wearing so many masks' phase of life, I was ignorant to the deep, dark stories I was telling myself. I knew that there was some serious BS going on within me, but I didn't know exactly what it was. There was so much going on it became a big, foggy mess.

I had to start listening and paying attention to the fog. I had to start shifting through those thoughts until I was able to identify the patterns.

Be clear in what you are actually saying to yourself in every situation. Be clear on what you believe regarding who you are, identify the stories you get lost in and be aware of what you actually feel or believe as a result of those stories.

I found the best way to gain back my power when I'm feeling emotional is to ask myself, "What am I thinking right now?"

Ask yourself this question and write down your answers. When your words slow down, ask yourself again, "What am I thinking right now?" Do not overanalyse anything at this point; the exercise is simply to get your thoughts out of your head and on paper. Every time you ask yourself this question, you will find your thoughts become deeper and deeper, to the point you might be embarrassed or ashamed to write down what you're actually thinking.

When this happens, give yourself a pat on the back, take a gulp of courage and write it down anyway. You are now one step closer to being able to own your BS!

Once you've cycled over "What am I thinking right now?" a number of times, you will likely 'feel' the root story has been identified. You might have a cry or physically feel lighter, but if you're really paying attention to the connection between your thoughts and body, you will sense you've hit the nail on the head. This is what we are looking for. Now it's identified, your next job is to put action behind it. We'll do the analysing of it later.

You've identified the big BS Story, so it's time to stop cycling by creating an action step of power. Ask yourself, "What can I do in this moment to bring my power back to me?"

Say you uncover that the big BS is "I feel like I'm not good enough". Then, due to years of habitual thinking, you start going into, "But why?" Your RAS is going to listen to this focus of "But why do I feel not good enough?" and show you all the examples it can of times in your life when you felt 'less than'. Failures, second bests, ridicules, opinions of others and judgements. The more evidence it shows you, the worse you feel. Before long, you won't look for an action because your focus lies solely on that story of "I feel like I'm not good enough". You're left feeling doubtful, insecure and yucky.

Consider the alternative. You identified "I feel like I'm not good enough" and your next thought is, "OK, what can I do about this, in this moment, that is going to bring power back to me?" Your RAS hears this and instead of looking for evidence to support the doubt, it looks for an answer to the question that is both supportive and proactive. "Go for a walk, get some fresh air and change what you're looking at." "Talk to a supportive friend/family member." "Remember when you achieved XYZ, you prepared that time, so let's do some preparation."

Considering these two alternatives, what option do you feel is going to leave you feeling powerful and in control?

Asking yourself "What am I thinking?" and "What can I do?" will provide you with an opportunity to depersonalise the situation and see something aside from what you are focusing on, giving you a different perspective and possible solution which helps you feel powerful.

Tip Time

1. Recognise how you might be generalising, deleting and distorting information. Look to see before you react.
2. Ask yourself, "What am I thinking?"
3. Followed by, "What can I do that will bring me a sense of power/control/choice?"
4. Do whatever proactive step you come up with!

CHAPTER 2

What am I saying to myself?

We cannot change what we are not aware of, and once we are aware we cannot help but change

Sheryl Sandberg

The desire to change any story is ignited with a single spark; an idea, possibility or single ray of hope saying, "Maybe it doesn't need to be this way". Sometimes a spark is subtle, other times it's obvious.

My spark happened when reality slapped me in the face and showed me what I was creating. After months of getting caught up in my BS and reacting as a result of the stories in my head, my reality caught up with me through Blair.

I was a loud, vocally out-of-control mumma for a little while and the physical aggression was starting to build. Until this point, I'd known my reactions were unnecessary and far from ideal, but I still lived in the ignorance it wasn't really impacting my children negatively.

One day, Blair and Alivia were playing quietly in the lounge room and I went in to watch and admire.

I walked up behind Blair to give him a pat on the back for encouragement, and instead of continuing to play, he flinched away from me. I'd dominated his world in such a way that his natural response was to flinch away from me!

I stopped dead in my tracks. "What the hell? How did this happen? Surely things hadn't been so bad he was now scared of me?"

At that moment, I knew if I didn't make significant changes, our entire future relationship would be strained, disconnected and not at all the experience he and I deserved.

My spark to change came as a sudden slap in the face. It still wasn't enough to get me to change. I had a way to go before rock bottom really pushed me into accepting my choices to change.

The spark was enough for me to start to recognise that my actions, which were fuelled largely by my thoughts, were in desperate need of attention.

It's important to recognise that regardless of your current situation there lies within you a spark which has the potential to create any life you desire. This spark is possibly currently lost, caught up and covered up by years of negative emotions, stories and thoughts dulling it down.

In my experience, women are afraid of change, mostly because we avoid things we don't know, including letting go of the BS that, while not serving us, keeps us in a comfortable box of 'this is me'.

If we are offered reassurance of what's on the other side, if we have confidence in the 'new' and in ourselves and opportunities available, change can be made easily. If there is a heap of BS going through your head supporting your feelings of doubt, unworthiness and insecurity, the idea of change is likely keeping you in a fairly frozen state.

Something has to happen, a catalyst so to speak, in order for us to warm to the idea that change is a good thing.

- An event that shakes you to the core, often coming in the form of a loss or significant health scare.
- A reflection of who you currently are slaps you in the face (as in my case), resulting in you not liking who you've become.
- A sense of dissatisfaction gets you to the point where you are sick and tired of feeling sick and tired.
- An event forces a sudden change, regardless of your desire or acceptance to change.
- A road block becomes apparent, teaching you a decision must be made to stay in the same cycle, experiencing and thinking the same things, or to grow, make an adjustment and do something different which allows for new experiences, thinking and possibilities.

'Making the change' can be an intimidating prospect as the definition of change is to make or become different. A sense of fear comes with 'changing' for it presents the possibility of becoming an entirely different person, losing the essence of who we are – those qualities we like about ourselves. It opens the possibility of "What if I don't like who I become?" With so many unknown factors, our focus centres around the negative outcomes, backed up by evidence provided from our unconscious mind, encouraging us to instead remain in the circumstances we are in, regardless of the BS.

Flip the lid on your thinking. Embrace the possibility of transforming, rather than changing. To 'transform' implies bettering who we already are, accepting, learning and growing.

Marylin Schirmer (my mentor and trainer from the Institute of Women International), discusses this in her book *The Maz Factor* (2011) "Change can imply 'different' to what you are right now, whereas to transform would be to stay you, but evolve, or improve to a better enhanced you, remaining your core self, only more of the core of yourself."

Doesn't it feel better to remain who you are, with less baggage and more strength?

I use the analogy of a staircase to describe this concept to my clients. Most of the women who come to me seek my help because they can no longer see 'new choices'; they are on a plateau leaving them dissatisfied, lost, stuck and limited. This analogy comes from one of my favourite quotes:

Every next level of your life will demand a different you.

~ Leonardo DiCaprio

Imagine your life as a staircase, each step representing a 'phase' of your life. The rise of a step is an opportunity where you 'stepped up' and made a conscious decision to do something different.

The widths of each step vary, depending on the circumstances of your life. Sometimes you are content cruising along for an extended period of time with how your life appears at the time.

Others are short lived, where the rise appears very quickly, as is the case for some relationships.

During the 'rise of the step', you transform, grow, and become a new, stronger, enhanced version of who you are. Sometimes, the rise is short and the transformation needed does not require much effort, thought or action. Other times, possibly like the one you are currently facing, leave you perplexed and feeling like you're standing at the base of a tall cliff, unable to see a way up yet seeking guidance, help and assistance to step up.

Regardless of the dimensions of your staircase, it represents your journey – your ability to see what needs adjusting, to make the change, to own the BS preventing you from moving up, to make the choices necessary to keep the journey moving along.

One thing each step has in common with every other step on your staircase is that it always has been and always will be your choice when you make the step. To transform, become aware, grow, evolve, step up and change.

CASE STUDY: Liz - Single, Self-Employed Woman

Liz believed she lived her life on her terms. Under closer observation, she was uncomfortable in her own skin, petrified of leaving home and having to put on the façade she felt was required of her. While she worked for herself, she couldn't see why people put value in the work she did, therefore she struggled to accept compliments or let people in to know the 'real Liz'. At her core, she felt unlovable, unworthy with no confidence or self-esteem.

In 2005, Liz was in an accident that left her with a head injury. This could have been the catalyst for her to turn her inner dialogue around. Instead Liz used it as a crutch, a reason to stay stuck in the set of circumstances which had become her life. She isolated herself, then felt sorry for herself as she was lonely and depressed. She turned to food for comfort, which only showed her how she was not in control herself. She was facing blood pressure medication and high amounts of pain medication.

In June 2016, Liz attended a group weekend focusing on goals and plans for the future. She left the weekend feeling completely lost and flat because she couldn't think of anything she wanted to achieve, nor felt she could achieve. After years of feeling unworthy, fake and thinking, "If people know who I really am, they want won't to know me", Liz came to the realisation she needed to transform. She was essentially fed up with herself.

After making the commitment to transform and grow, Liz now has normal blood pressure, takes less medication and is losing weight in a healthy way. She is out of the house, her business has picked up and she involves herself in the world around her, cultivating friendships that are nurturing and genuine. "I know that I am loved for who I am now, and that I am enough. I've learned to use the strategies Bree taught me for myself, and to take the time for myself to re-charge as needed. Without taking the chance on myself, to be truly honest and ready to change, I would just be a shell of who I'm supposed to be. I LIKE me now"

Liz's story is a spectacular example of the desire to make a change, transform and grow. Her example teaches us this decision is a process. For years, Liz lived in a space of powerlessness and nothing would change long term for her until she made the choice to claim back her power.

Every situation and thought you have will fall into one of two categories:

'Blame, Powerlessness and Victim' or 'Responsibility, Power and Victor'.

You know you are blaming a situation or person if your energy is flat, down, negative and 'outside of you'. Your inner dialogue will begin focusing on negative stories and looking for more details within that story.

"I just don't understand why this is happening to me!"

"Why did he pick her?"

"Why is she better than me?"

"Why do they always do that?"

"Why did he say that to me? Why is he such a..."

"Why does my child have to be sick? Why can't there be a cure?"

Victim mode, as many refer to it, will look for the 'why' in a scenario, believing that the story has the answers. Asking or focusing on the why is going to keep you circling in the story. It is code for your brain to analyse for more detail, which is not going to change the event or outcome.

Look at what I was saying to myself in 2012: I was in complete victim mode, blaming my son for the situation I felt I was living.

For women, this is dangerous as the more time we spend in that story, the more emotion we connect to it and the more emotionally foggy the situation will appear. Remember those filters. Every time you recycle your story, you are running the story through filters which further generalise, distort and delete information from the real event.

By contrast, responsibility and power choices will focus on solutions. The story won't change no matter how many times it is revisited, so instead of looking for 'the missing clue' a victor will look for learning.

"OK, so this happened, it sucks, what can I do about it right now?"

"I hate that my child is sick, but what are my options? I can a) learn about alternatives or b) focus on making the most of each day, creating memories."

"I didn't get that promotion. What areas can I improve on for next time? Maybe I could ask for some feedback?"

"What was I trying to achieve by having that argument? What could I say differently next time to explain myself better?"

In the case of arguments, you might ask, "What is more important to me right now: being right and proving my point, or having my own peace of mind intact?"

These do not disregard the negative. In each case the emotion is acknowledged and felt, however, rather than setting up camp and staying in this zone, a victor will look outside of what they are focusing on then redirect their energy and improve the situation as best they can.

Anytime you become aware of a negative emotion or thought pattern, build on the previous two questions from the last chapter, "What am I thinking right now?" and "What can I do to bring my power back to me?"

Ask yourself things such as "What can I learn?" "What can I do differently?" "What one action is going to take me to a more neutral or positive state?"

Each of these questions are 'what' (or 'how') questions and they send your unconscious mind into a search for answers.

There are 6 Stages of moving from a state of powerlessness to power.

Act	Ownership	Power
Acknowledge	Careful	
Accept	Responsibility	
Recognise	Truth	
Refusal	Denial	
Removed	Blame	Powerlessness

Removed

You feel removed from your power. Your natural instinct is to blame someone or something exterior to you for why you feel what you feel and why you are where you are. You don't believe there is an option or possibility for you to change because it's someone else's fault. Their actions or the fallout of such resulted in you being where you are now. For the majority of you reading this book, I'm happy to say it's unlikely you are resonating here. People who live in this zone tend not to look for self-help books to improve their life; instead they rely on other people to rescue them or create a change of circumstance for them.

Although there will be circumstances where you find yourself slipping back into a removed state. When you do, there's no need to beat yourself up – it's life. To bring yourself back from this state, ask yourself a question such as, "Where is my power lying now and what can I do to take ownership of my place in this space?"

Refusal

You recognised you were blaming and looking for options outside the current situation but a large element in your thinking believes change can't occur. Therefore, you are in a state of denial.

Denial is more about believing that although there might be an option to change, you don't believe you can make it happen. This belief is often formed through a lack of self-worth or value, e.g. "I don't have what it takes to make that change", "I'm not strong enough", or lack of knowledge about the situation. You take what little you do know and make a decision based on that, without exploring it further.

Some of you may be at a stage of denial. You picked up this book because you're sick and tired of feeling like you do, but your BS or inner dialogue is turned up loud, telling you it's not possible.

In this case, ask yourself questions such as:

"What is the purpose of me believing I don't have a choice?"

"Where am I limiting myself and what can I do to move above, or around that limitation?"

"What could happen if I did make a different choice and follow through with it?"

"What will happen if I don't?"

The answers to these questions will help you identify what is really going on here, where your self-value lies and what fears are hiding amongst your current thoughts.

Recognise

The recognize stage is becoming aware that to regain your personal power is to recognise and begin to be open to the possibility; that regardless of how difficult it might seem, you can change the reality of what is going on. It's about seeing the truth for what it is, seeing your role in the current situation, your behaviour and storytelling, then being ok with it.

This stage of powerless to power can be confronting, but with it comes the greatest potential for ownership.

The first time I acknowledged my reoccurring thought of "I hate being a mum" I felt physically sick. What kind of woman was I? I hated myself so much for that thought and for a time, I spiralled back into a space of denial. I wasn't ready to move past it. I had to "sit in my shit" until I was ready to own it.

At this stage of owning your power, if you feel fear bubbling up and freezing you, my suggestion is to question it. For example:

"OK, I hear what I'm saying to myself. Although it's confronting, I'm going to work through it. Is this thought truth? Is there any evidence to support the opposite of what I am thinking?"

For example, when I recognised "I hate being a mum" I looked for examples in my life where I loved being a mum. The snuggles, giggles, and 'I love yous'. the more I looked for a new 'truth', the more frequent these truths would appear.

Accept

As you move into the phase of power, you accept responsibility. You accept that for every situation you're involved in, you are the only person you're responsible for in terms of how you give and receive information. You not only identify what you are saying, but you believe it at a deep level. In this moment of accepting responsibility, you will be more efficient at owning your BS and working through it.

From this stage of acceptance, you can deliberately choose what you do and how you behave, react and respond to a degree. I'll explain more about this in later chapters, however it's a good time to let you know this new acceptance still requires you to consciously choose a different path, which at times will seem near impossible. Remember you have years of stories fuelled by years of emotions; at times you will react with emotion before thinking about your place in the story. The more often you accept and choose a different path, the less time you will spend in the negative, 'no options' state.

Acknowledge

Showing careful acknowledgement for your decisions, the good, bad and instinctual reactions will help you move through challenges without getting caught up in them. It's about acknowledging your Female Factor - your female way of processing emotions and situations, while acknowledging you are doing the best you can in every situation that comes your way.

For example, knowing more about your personal cycle and how your hormones impact your emotional reactions will help you carefully navigate certain situations without too much self-criticism. Being able to acknowledge your triggers so you can prepare yourself for interactions and events will allow you to maintain a more stable space of ownership, calm and confidence.

Act

In the last stage, you begin to live with ownership on a more consistent basis. To me, this is the definition of Emotional Confidence™. It allows you to be whatever you need to be, knowing you can hang onto the story, let it go, address it or live with. You choose how you act and you have complete ownership, which is the ultimate personal power.

This is very important! There will be situations in your life, stories that will drag you into an emotional fog that you will want to sit in for a bit. My unconscious mind was not ready to let go of "I hate being a mum" immediately as there were lessons I had to learn before I could address it. I had to sit in my shit, process the truth of it, gain new perspectives, then when I was ready to address it. In that time, ownership was absolute key. Anytime I tried to push it away and ignore it, it would rear its ugly head, reminding me there was no escaping it.

Now that you know the progression of stages, let's break it down into 3 easily manageable steps.

Step One - See the Truth

What is really going on? What are you saying to yourself? What thoughts and stories are you are getting caught in? What is the reality of the situation you're getting lost in?

Seeing the truth is confronting. You are ripping the band-aid off, exposing the raw skin beneath. In order for you to have complete ownership and power, it is imperative you begin to identify and see the real truth.

One great way of doing this is in your journal. Start writing and scribble it out. Your thoughts will appear before your eyes the more often you do this. I'll be sharing more about why this is such a powerful thing to do in the next chapter, because the deeper and more often you dig to find out what is really going on at an unconscious level, the more you will learn about your BS.

You can dig deeper by asking yourself any of the previously recommended questions and writing down your answers. Each question will take your thoughts deeper than the last.

Step Two - Start to Analyse What You've Written Down

The more honest you are with your analysing, the more you look for the truth, fear and distortion of filters, the more you will be able to see where you can change the patterns. Analysing is exciting as it allows you to see what your triggers are. Your triggers are going to be people or situations outside your control causing you to react or feel a particular way. Often the triggers cannot be changed, however with awareness of a trigger you can start to prepare yourself to respond instead of react.

Step Three - Create a New Truth

Identify what you are going to do to gain the change or results you want from this situation. Put your plan in place and start doing it one step at a time.

Tip Time

1. Pay attention to what you're focusing on. Are you looking for details by asking yourself 'why' questions or do you look for solutions? You can put your brain into search-and-solve mode with 'what' questions such as "What can I learn?" "What can I do differently?" "What do I want?"
2. See the truth. Keep a journal, knowing it is a safe space to spill your beans. Start to see what you are truly thinking, feeling and experiencing.
3. Analyse your text in a way that allows you to look for the lessons and strengths. Acknowledge your triggers so you can respond instead of react.
4. Write a new truth by setting up a plan with action steps you can implement to achieve the results you want.

CHAPTER 3

Connection between your thoughts and your body

Words are containers for power.
You choose what kind of power they carry

Joyce Meyer

It's 2am. You wake in a sweat, heart beating rapidly as you blink back tears.

Did that really happen?

Or was it a dream?

You're confused.

It felt so real, you can still see the nightmare playing in your mind.

You get out of bed to grab a drink of water and as you walk down the dark hallway, your eye catches a glimpse of something dark on the wall.

Shit. Is that a spider?

You jump. Your heart skips another beat. You hate spiders!

No, the kids have just left a handprint on the wall.

As your heart starts to calm you recognise your head is playing games with you, yet your body has responded as if the events were real.

This is the power of the mind/body story connection and what we are going to explore in depth throughout this chapter.

Every thought you have, be it an imagined event, a replayed version of a past story or a current perception of right now, creates an image in your mind which in turn provides your body with all the senses, the sights, sounds, feelings and information required for a physical response.

Test this theory for yourself.

Close your eyes and recall a moment in your life where you have been with a really good girlfriend and something happened causing you both to laugh. A full hoot of joy, tears streaming down your faces, rolling back and forth, a snort or gurgle of uncontrollable happiness. Side-splitting fun making your cheeks hurt from smiling. In your mind's eye, see that moment. Feel the contentment, friendship, joy and happiness within your body. Where do you feel that? How do you describe this memory?

Wipe the memory clear and think of a time when you nursed a brand-new baby, maybe your child, or a child of someone special to you. Feel the squishy bundle of joy in your arms. Feel the warmth. See the look of innocence on the baby's face. Feel their little hands in yours, pudgy fingers grasping your fingers. Hear the tiny little noises coming from the child. Feel what you felt in that moment: love, tenderness, protectiveness, admiration. Where in your body do you feel those emotions? How do you describe this memory?

In these examples, just like in a nightmare or dream that wakes you, you have used your imagination to recreate past events. They are no longer real, and yet in all scenarios, your brain created an image and in turn your body reacted with happiness, joy, love, tenderness, anger and pain.

This is important for women to know because the more time we spend thinking about and replaying memories or events of the past, the stronger the emotions connected to those events become. This is inherently why we find it so hard to 'let things go'!

In my early 20s, my best friend and I had a disagreement. To this date, I have no idea what the argument was about, however I remember being completely consumed by the events both leading up to the argument and the argument itself. At every opportunity, I talked about it. I found reasons to talk about her and hash out my side of the story to whomever would listen. Aaron would frequently say to me, "Bree, just let it go, she's probably not even thinking about it or you, so why are you letting it upset you?" Logically, I knew what he was saying was right. But I couldn't move past what happened.

I was absolutely consumed by this silly little argument. The pain, hurt and betrayal I felt as a result of it continued to charge my inability to let it go.

When I went through the 'crazy, psycho mumma' period, I would lay in bed of a night, rehashing the day, playing over in my head all the things I said and did, the conversations, arguments and over-the-top reactions. As I did, I would feel guiltier, angrier, more ashamed and overwhelmed, then less and less worthy of being a mum, a wife and a business owner. Every night the same story played, and it left me feeling drained each morning when I awoke.

I began to refer to these moments as the 'emotional fog', because that's how I felt; I was living life caught up in a mass of memories, thoughts and stories. I was living with my head in the clouds, but unlike soft, fluffy white clouds of positivity, they were dark storm clouds, building in intensity.

I began to heavily rely on journaling to clear my head and break down the stories. In fact, journaling is still one of my favourite things to do which I recommend to my clients.

Why Is Journaling So Powerful?

There are a multitude of studies that have shown the emotional release from journaling lowers anxiety and stress, inducing better sleep. Dr James Pennebaker, author of Writing to Heal (2004, New Harbinger Publications) notes that the physical act of writing down our thoughts gives us the ability to create space to recognise, analyse and recreate the thoughts that aren't serving us to be more neutral or positive. This is because during the act of writing, the left hemisphere of the brain is accessed, the part of that brain that is typically analytical and rational. So while your left brain is busy getting down the details, the right, more emotional and intuitive part of your brain (the more dominant part of the brain for most females) is left to feel. Together, your mental blocks are removed, allowing your brain power to process the thoughts with more understanding and insight.

I love journaling because it gives me an insight into what I'm actually saying to myself. It allows me to see, on paper, the energy of my thoughts and neutralise this intensity in a simple, easy way. To determine how much truth lies within my thoughts, and how much BS I'm actually creating.

Assume I've had a hard day. The kids argued, I overreacted once or twice and things in my business aren't progressing how I want them to. I go to bed feeling frustrated, guilty and insecure. I might write something like:

Today was a shit day. The kids were at each other's throats all the time – I'm so sick and tired of the whining and whining. Why can't they just get along like normal kids?
At one point, I got so angry I screamed at them to shut up, which was bloody stupid because afterwards I felt like the worst mum in the world.
I know I was reacting to them out of frustration because I really wanted to do more in my business today and I didn't – I was lazy and kept getting distracted. Seriously, I don't know why I bother. I know I can't do this.
I guess tomorrow I'll just try and make more phone calls and try not to lose my shit.

Nine times out of 10, I'll feel better purely through getting these thoughts onto paper. If I want to take it one step further, to not just 'get it out' but to actually deal with it, I'll spend a few moments analysing it from a proactive standpoint.

I take note of the 'feel' of what I've written. The above feels flat, frustrated and limited – not at all uplifting or encouraging.

Next, I'll identify what 'lies' I'm telling myself. How much of my recap of the day has been misconstrued and made up? How much is actual truth?

Lies in the above example include:

- 'All the time'. Nothing happens all the time, except breathing.
- The second lie is 'normal kids'. There is no such thing as normal, so this lie is setting up an unrealistic expectation.
- 'Worst mum in the world' is another lie. This is a perception and regardless of how you interpret your mothering skills, it's highly improbable you are the worst mother in the world. In fact, it shows more how you feel about yourself and speaks volumes regarding the message you are feeding yourself. If you feel this way, it's important you start to reconstruct the way you see yourself. You're doing the best you can, so start saying "I'm a good mum doing the best I can!"
- 'Lazy' is another lie. I'm fairly confident you are not lazy. If you have a job, a relationship, friendships, children, a home, hobbies, tasks you do any time of the day, and you do even 1 of them, you are not lazy. Stop speaking so unkindly about yourself and change the story to "I do the best I can".
- "I know I can't do this!" Yep, it's another lie. Reality is, we are never 100% certain of what we can or can't do. We cannot be 100% certain what tomorrow will bring. Some things you do know, such as your name and birthday for instance, and we can be certain that there are challenges we need to overcome. However, we can never be absolutely certain of an outcome.

Next, I go through the page and circle all the red flag words and replace them with either a neutral or positive version. I call these neutral or positive words 'white words'!

Red flag words include negative emotional words, words which limit my thinking, such as:

All/Never/All of them/None of them/Always: These words are general words, making a situation or population more definitive, cancelling out options. In the above example "all the time" is an over-exaggeration. It's also an example of a 'lie' that I'm telling myself. The reality is kids argue from time to time, however, not all the time. Instead of using a general word or phrase such as "all the time", give yourself a reality check and keep it in perspective.

Why: Why is a word that looks for more detail and information. It keeps us cycling in the story, trying to make sense of something with no answer. Instead of looking for the why by asking why questions, ask yourself a what or how question instead. How and what questions are solution and action focused, which help solve the issues and train your brain to look for solutions in other areas of your life.

Don't: Don't isn't processed by the brain, so instead of processing "I don't know why I bother!" your brain hears "Why bother?" Do your best to eliminate "don't" from your vocabulary.

Can't/Try: These are two words which set us up for failure or an easy way out of a challenge. If you believe you "can't", you're telling yourself you can't, simple as that. If it's something you really want to do, be confident with "I can!"

I'll try not to: Likewise, this is a lack of commitment to what you want to do. Yoda says, "Do, or do not, there is no try!" and I agree. Respect your wishes enough to commit to what you want to do: "tomorrow I will" or "I'm not going to do that". It feels secure at your core when you do it too.

(Funny realisation: you run into a girlfriend downtown and say, "We'll have to try and catch up!" and you know the moment those words come out, you won't. So why not respect her and your own time by being honest? Say, "As much as I'd love to catch up properly, I'm really busy at the moment, however when things settle down I'll get in touch.")

But: This is a word the brain doesn't process properly. Everything said prior to the word 'But' is essentially deleted from your brain's filter.

"I love you but I hate when you argue with me," is heard as "I hate when you argue with me," which, to a young child, or insecure doubt-filled woman can simply become "I hate you!" "You did a good job but next time you'll need to..." The brain doesn't hear the praise, only the adjustment that's required, which can be quickly internalised as "I'm not good enough."

Where possible, use 'however' instead of 'but'. However allows for the entire message to be processed. Alternatively, learn to structure your sentences in a way that allows but to act as an emphasis for your meaning, e.g. "You made a mistake here BUT I appreciate the effort you go to."

Let's restructure the previous journal entry example using positive or neutrally charged emotional words and some of our new white words. It's a good thing to note that the new structure doesn't need to make logical sense. Remember your brain doesn't 'see' the grammar, it sees the overall picture created with the energy and words.

Today was a ~~shit~~ good day. The kids were at each other's throats ~~all~~ only some of the day (or maybe I'd rewrite this whole sentence to say 'The kids were good to each other most of day') – I'm so ~~sick and tired~~ appreciative of the ~~whinging~~ laughing and ~~whining~~ playing, ~~why can't they~~ I love that they just get along like ~~normal~~ kids. At one point, I got so ~~angry~~ happy that I ~~screamed~~ laughed at them to ~~shut up~~ play, which was bloody ~~stupid~~ smart because afterwards I just felt like the ~~worst~~ best mum in the world. I know that I was reacting to them out of ~~frustration~~ appreciation because I really wanted to do more in my business today and I ~~didn't~~ did what I could – I was ~~lazy~~ proactive and kept getting ~~distracted~~ enthusiastic in ~~shit~~ tasks. Seriously, I ~~don't~~ know why I bother, I know I ~~can't~~ can do this! I guess tomorrow I'll just ~~try and~~ make more phone calls and I'll ~~try not to lose my shit~~ do what I can.

How much better does that feel? It might not be 100% accurate. Remember, the body believes whatever the mind sees, so when we paint a new picture of our day, our body responds by feeling the appropriate emotions, in this case, content, happy and calm. As the newly structured paragraph is written within the realms of possible, your brain will likely accept it easily.

CASE STUDY: Leanne, Married

Mother of 2 Adult Children, Mortgage Broker and Active Carer for Her Elderly Parents (Both with Alzheimer's)

Prior to owning her BS, Leanne felt lost, anxious, depressed and broken. She felt she was on the verge of losing her family and friends, and as a result, her professional work was suffering. She was living in a state of blame; everyone else was responsible for the lack of love and happiness in her life. She frequently yelled at her family and had daily confrontations with her work colleagues. She hated her life and her job and resented her family and husband.

This battle had been with Leanne for many years. She had sought help from various counsellors, psychologists and support groups. From this help, she believed she loved herself at some level, however still struggled to feel love for herself on a regular basis.

She had no focus, clarity or direction. She lost faith in her ability to make decisions, leaving her feeling overwhelmed, frustrated, impatient, and misunderstood.

Physically, Leanne suffered chest pains from anxiety, throat restrictions and regular 'croaky' voices. She was fatigued and experienced regular indigestion, gout, leg cramps and insomnia. To counteract all this, she was addicted to shopping, eating and alcohol – addictions she used to reward herself when she felt happy, and to soothe herself when she was sad.

Leanne was trapped in a state where the stories she told herself, and the world she perceived as a result of these stories, left her feeling empty. Once Leanne took ownership of the BS, she gained back her happiness and direction. She knows at her core she has the capabilities and strength to do what she hopes and dreams for. "I now feel like I own the universe. My family and I are connected on a much higher level – love and acceptance feels so natural and real to me! I look after myself now – regularly meditating, using positive affirmations and visualisations to power through challenges. I'm so much more aware of how I talk to myself – I can't believe those old stories had so much hold over me – or, more to the point, that I allowed them! When BS comes in now, I work through it with purpose. I know that I will continue to grow from everything with power and wisdom from within."

The stories we tell ourselves can make or break us. Our power comes from our commitment to becoming aware of what those stories are and making adjustments to neutralise the negative intensity by offering new possibilities.

Courage is sometimes required, as 'hearing' those thoughts for the first time can be confronting. During the time I was owning my BS, I kept a piece of paper handy at all times. Whenever I felt myself start to get emotional, I took note of what was going on. My paper looked like this:

What am I doing?	What am I thinking?	What am I feeling?	What can I do?
E.g: Trying to make phone calls.	E.g: She's going to say no, or think I'm pushy.	E.g: Nervous, insecure, not good enough.	E.g: Make the call anyway. Write a script out first. Be prepared.
E.g: Making dinner.	E.g: I am such a bad cook, I'm a bad wife and mum. They deserve better.	E.g: Not good enough.	E.g: Take a breath, follow the recipe. It's all a learning curve.
E.g: Putting kids to bed.	E.g: I hate this. Why can't they just do as they are told.	E.g: Angry. Tired. Exhausted.	E.g: Ask Aaron for help.

As I did this, I became aware of my thoughts in the moment and started to have more ownership. You'll see the last column finished with a proactive 'what' question, this stopped me dwelling on how I felt, over-analysing negative aspects of the experience, replaying the story and creating more emotional charge around the event.

With dedication and commitment to the journey, I changed my thoughts and looked for things I could do differently. When it came to my nightly routine of journaling, I recalled specifics rather than overworked, over-told interpretations of what I thought happened.

I journaled religiously. On nights I didn't, I tossed and turned, struggling to sleep as I rehashed every part of the day, beat myself up, then woke up feeling exhausted. On nights I allowed myself 5 or 10 minutes to get my thoughts out of my head and onto paper, I slept peacefully and woke with determination to have control.

Similar to over-thinking, there is risk of over-writing, getting caught up in the negative space of your head, so you need to create boundaries around journaling. My hard and fast rule is once I've reworked a page, that's it. I can't go over it again that night or the next day. I'll go back and read my learnings to grow from the experiences if need be at a future date, but that's all.

Creating awareness around what you're actually saying to yourself is going to provide you with more clarity than before. The jumbled mess of emotional foggy BS will start to clear, allowing choices, power and possibilities to return to your life. The most important thing to know is you are in the driver's seat; this is your journey, it's your commitment to yourself. The decision to take ownership lies in your hands. Are you going to take it?

Tip Time:

1. Download and print the tracking sheets accompanying this book, available for free at http://tinyurl.com/oybs-downloads
2. Track your actions, thoughts and feelings. Throughout the day, look for things you can do in the moment to put power back into your hands.
3. Create a daily ritual of dumping your thoughts before you go to sleep at night. To keep journaling proactive, I suggest the following:
    a. Use a two-page spread where the left-hand side represents the 'dumping' of your thoughts. It's the current reality as you are experiencing it and seeing it right now. The right-hand side is the positive side, use to learn or become aware. (See Step d.)
    b. Limit the time you actually spend writing – I personally give myself a 5-10-minute time frame to free write my thoughts using no more than the single two-page spread.
    c. Don't edit as you write; simply let the words flow out onto the paper. Once done, work back through what you wrote with the Red Flag/White Word exercise
    d. Use the right-hand side as the positive page. Make note of what you learned or became aware of as a result of free writing. List 3 moments you found appreciation and gratitude for throughout the day and 3 things you appreciate about yourself, or 3 wins so to speak.
4. Finish your day giving yourself a pat on the back. You've did the best you could and it was more than enough.

CHAPTER 4

Understanding the female brain and hormones

Our generation is becoming so busy trying to prove that women can do what men can do that women are losing their uniqueness. Women weren't created to do everything a man can do. Women were created to do everything a man can't do

unknown

The most significant thing I learned on my journey of personal development is the ability to embrace my Female Factor, and the ease, influence and self-compassion that comes as a result of working in a way natural to me, as a female.

What Is the Female Factor?

The Female Factor is understanding how your brain process, stores and recognises emotions. It is acknowledging and working with the different abilities of the female brain, understanding the connection between your emotions and hormones and tapping into your natural instincts and intuition – trusting you know what is right for you.

Let's break it down, starting with the female brain. This information will resonate with approximately 90% of females and 10% of males. As with everything in life, there is no black and white when it comes to females.

I shared with you the fact that the female brain has up to 25% more connection with the female heart than males have. With more blood flow throughout our brain at any given moment, we revisit emotional memories more often than men.

When an event happens and an emotion is assigned to the event, the memory is essentially burned into our brain to be recalled at any given time. As females, we do this more often than men because the main energy fuelling us is emotion over reason and logic.

For example, if you recall the day you met your partner, you likely remember a more detailed version of events then if you were to ask your partner to recall the same moment. He might have a vague description of what you looked like, what you wore, something that was said. He might be able to describe his emotion as happy or nervous. He probably won't remember much about what was said, how long it took to share a kiss or what was said afterwards. It's an important event in his life but he hasn't assigned the same level of emotional attachment to it.

You probably remember exactly what you were wearing, how your hair was, how he was dressed, what was said, how long the conversation lasted, the undercurrent of emotions, energy and more. This is because you've not just assigned nervous and happy to the memory, but lust, excitement and a myriad of other emotions, well and truly burning this moment into your memory bank.

In your professional and personal life, with success or failure, positive or negative experiences, there are numerous examples when you, as a female, have assigned a number of emotions to an event that meant something to you because you're naturally more emotional mind processes events according to how it makes you feel. Those events are stored as 'something significant', regardless of how 'significant' it really is, hence the issue with emotional assignment. Our brain thinks anything with an emotion must be kept for later use, even if it's something that really doesn't impact or make a difference to your life experience.

Test this theory for yourself. Recall a moment in your life you deem to be an important moment such as a job promotion, goal you achieved, something to do with your partner's business or career, your business or career or something to do with one of your children. Allow yourself to recall all the details you can, then ask your partner to do the same. I will bet that although he may remember some vague details, he will be stumped when you really start questioning him.

With emotional events, men's more logical brains seek to make logical sense of the event rather than looking for further detail. Once they make a connection that sits well in their heads, "Oh, that's why this happened!" they are often able to move on and let it go.

We, as women, are so focused on details and emotions, trying to understand every tiny aspect of the event, we create more drama, more emotional connections and therefore ultimately have more difficulties letting it go and moving on.

It's interesting to recall the number of emotions you assign to these events and how you describe them to yourself compared to how your partner describes them. Women have larger limbic systems than men. The limbic system is a complex system of nerves and networks in the brain, involving several areas near the edge of the cortex concerned with instinct and mood. It controls basic emotions (fear, pleasure, anger) and drives (hunger, sex, dominance, care of offspring).

As a result, women are more in touch with their emotional selves and better able to express themselves emotionally. For every 'happy' a man feels, women can feel anything from joy to excitement, love to content or enthusiastic to blissed out. Men will describe 'angry' as pissed off or fed up; women will describe it as losing my shit, being out of control, angry, frustrated, pissed off, fed up, over it and whatever else floats our boats. The verbal centres in both hemispheres of our brains give us the ability to describe our emotions much like the spectrum of colours with a million different variations, combinations and possibilities to describe how we feel, think and experience things. Men, with their smaller limbic systems and left-hemisphere-only verbal centre, will generally stick to the basics. If something can be said with less words, you can guarantee a man will opt for the simpler version.

This ability to verbalise is accentuated by our ability to multitask, something made easier for us because of the extra white matter within our brains. We are designed to do more than one thing at a time. We can have a conversation with someone, while thinking about what we need to do next and what we haven't gotten around to doing yet, while sipping on a cup of coffee, criticising our food choices and watching the kids all while tapping our foot to the song on the radio. While beneficial in many cases, it results in limited down time. This is reserved for the 'quiet' time of our cycle (more on that soon). Understanding this will give you more control and allowance when it comes to your 'busyness'.

Men, try as they might, are not equipped for multitasking because they have more grey matter in their brains. They are naturally single-focused, tunnel-visioned, one-thing-at-a-time creatures.

The next time you leave your partner with a big, detailed list of things you'd like him to do (without writing it all down) and he forgets, realise he's not doing it on purpose. His brain literally doesn't have the ability to focus on more than one thing at a time. When you're leaving instructions for him, his brain is focusing all its energy on listening to you, not necessarily becoming aware of what you are saying and requesting of him!

While we're at it, when you jump from one topic to the next, quickly changing the direction and point of your conversation and your partner gets completely lost, appearing not to care, know it's likely not because he doesn't care. Instead, it has to do with the fact his brain can't keep up! Slow down, take a breath, and give the poor bugger a chance to catch up before changing topics!

One fascinating thing about the male brain is their ability to de-compartmentalise their memories and different aspects in their brains. This means they categorise everything that happens in their lives into a series of well-planned segments, each segment separate from the one next to it, with little or no possibility of the segments crossing and combining. One of these segments, the 'nothing box' as Mark Gungor, International Marriage Counsellor and expert on male and female brains calls it, is a space where men can go to at any time of the day, during any event, that allows them to completely tune out from what is going on around them.

Women's brains are not at all segmented; our brains are like a ball of wire where everything is connected to everything and it's all charged with emotion, keeping it buzzing 24 hours a day. At the end of this chapter I provide an easy, effective tool that can slow your thinking, giving you the opportunity to create more space, clarity and calm.

These differences are some of approximately 100 gender differences in the brain that help us understand ourselves and the opposite sex from a neurological perspective, and help us acknowledge why addressing problems that stem predominantly from the brain and mind need to be approached differently for both sexes.

Personally, the day I learned these things, when I accepted these differences between my brain and Aaron's brain, was the day I saw see him through a different set of lenses. I was no longer as quick to judge him; instead I recognised he just really loved his nothing box, as so many men do!

Instead of getting upset when he couldn't keep up with my storytelling which bounced from bills, to our kids, to my business, family, friends and back again in 5 minutes, I was able to slow down and give him time to process what I was saying, which helped me to go from constant overwhelm and 'busy' to slow and calm myself. Nothing seems urgent when you're not bouncing from one thing to the next!

I explained myself in ways that helped him understand me better and allowed me to process what I was thinking and feeling in a more controlled manner.

My reactions didn't change overnight. What changed quickly was my ability to recognise what was going on from a different perspective. I was able to understand him, see the situation from his point of view and accept things for how they were, not how I thought they were.

CASE STUDY: Magali – De Facto Partner,

Mother of 3 Boys, Operations Leader in the Manufacturing Industry, Coach

As the primary financial provider for her family, Magali lived with high levels of stress, overwhelm and guilt that she was not enough for her boys because she was away from the home working. The BS she told herself was fed by the perception she had from others, that to be a good mum she had to be a 'stay-at-home mum'.

She was living in fear at work, so worried about being seen incompetent that she rarely spoke up, believing she would be judged and seen as 'not good enough' by her peers, who were predominantly male. This constant replay of worrying what people thought of her became a self-fulfilling prophecy. A performance feedback report at work indicated management was concerned about her abilities to do her role; she was no longer portraying the qualities of leadership and personal development which landed her the job. With that, the fear of not being enough for her work or her family, became a real concern. Every night she replayed events from work, beating herself up over what she felt she should have done and said differently.

This kept her from 'being present' at home. Every night at home, she was physically present, never really emotionally present because she was so caught up in her head, with worries and doubts about herself. "I'm not good enough, I'm an imposter, I'm not competent, I'm selfish, I can't do it, it's too hard, it always happens to me, they all know and think I will not make it, I've screwed it up, they will find out, it's my fault, he is feeling bad because of me." This was the dialogue of Magali's BS and it impacted her family, her work colleagues and her team because she wasn't able to live life according to her full potential.

Since Magali took ownership of BS, she recognised the power of her inner strength, knowing the BS is merely a perception of a situation she can address at any time. "I am so happy now, joyful, light, grounded and determined. My family is happy, we enjoy meaningful discussions now.

At work, I speak up. I have a strong confidence and strong voice that I've haven't previously been able to muster. I am so in touch with who I am as a woman, and what I can offer to my role because of that. I share and actively participate with passion – even my CEO is now recognising the efforts and has praised me in my confidence and the impact this is making on others. I am having fun with what I am doing and my goals now seem easy and achievable."

What's blatantly obvious with the Female Factor is our hormones. Not many women recognise the deep connection between our hormones and our emotional states. Both fuel one another, yet if you address only one you still feel out of whack. Approach both of them to create balance with your emotions and hormones then life becomes that much easier to create and navigate.

Few women really appreciate that regardless of where you are in life, between infancy and death, your hormones are on a constantly changing course of increasing and decreasing. As such, everything we do, how we behave, think, feel, sleep and eat are affected by these hormone fluctuations.

Traditionally speaking, we are taught that a cycle in the life of a woman revolves purely around our period, which, as a by-product means for many women who don't get a regular period, have ceased having periods or use a form of contraception that stops periods, they create a belief that "I don't have a period therefore I don't have a cycle."

This narrow view of a cycle shouldn't impact our days or lives any more than absolutely necessary. I remember being told by our PE teacher that having our periods and cramps didn't excuse us from doing activity and instead of resting and nurturing our bodies, we should push past the pain and go for a run.

That's crap! Women can cause themselves physical and emotional damage by 'pushing through' that time of the month instead of listening to and honouring our natural need to take things easy.

This is partially due to the many years society has functioned on the more masculine, linear way of living life, during the Industrial Age in particular. The time of structure, systems and 'full steam ahead' slowly but surely tried to make the Female Factor take a back step in our very female ways.

Thankfully, it is becoming more commonly known and accepted that rest and nurture are the appropriate ways to address 'that time of the month'. Our hormonal fluctuations mean we, as females, are not linear but very cyclic humans. There is a time within each cycle for every activity we expect of ourselves and every day is not one of them!

During this chapter, I share with you the key phases occurring during the rise and fall of your hormone levels and how that plays out for your life from month to month. The information shared is based on a traditional 28-day cycle, however it is important for you to know your own cycle, including the length, intensity and symptoms which change from woman to woman. As such, begin tracking your cycle and what it means to you. Of course, there are variations which can alter your personal symptoms, including hormone imbalances or physically stressful situations. Keep your life circumstances in mind as you read as this will give you a fairly clear overview to use as a baseline.

I was introduced to the concept of a 4-phase cycle by the 2009 book *The Optimised Woman* by Miranda Gray. If you find the information I share with you valuable, then this book will guide you through a thorough explanation of what to expect within a cycle and how to create your ideal life over your cycle.

To make sense of the phases of your cycle, you can relate each phase to the seasons of the year, i.e. your winter becomes days 1-7 of your cycle, which is traditionally when a period might be experienced. Spring spans days 8-14, which turns into summer for days 15-21 and finishes with autumn for Days 22-28.

Let's explore these four phases in more detail.

Winter: Days 1-7

Winter is the reflective phase of your cycle. This can be an emotionally flat time, a time where all you want to do is withdraw and hibernate from the world. It's the perfect time to slow down and give yourself permission to stop instead of constantly pushing through.

Slow down physically, mentally and emotionally. At this time, your awareness turns inward and feelings can be at their most intense as your connection with the subconscious is at its strongest. If you are in tune with yourself, you may find this phase of your cycle is similar to a meditation. You'll be more accepting of letting go of worries and concerns, mostly because you couldn't be bothered with the emotional or physical effort it takes to care. You might daydream more; allow it to happen as great ideas can be born at this time.

You want to sleep more, have less energy and a lower capacity to process complex ideas. It's a time of restoration and renewal of energies; as such it is a great time to make and commit to change.

Unfortunately, for many women, family, social and work demands put us in a position where we need to 'soldier on'. Forcing yourself to be more active mentally can have detrimental effects, generating anger, frustration and stress. It is important for you to find ways of dealing with the reality of your demands so you are supporting your body. Where possible, plan your activities around the dynamic phase of your cycle of spring and summer (see below), to accommodate this slower time. During the winter phase, take the pressure off yourself to perform and just focus on what you can do.

If you find yourself in a rigid role during winter, give yourself a 2-3 minute break every half hour or so. Use these few minutes to calm your breath, create space in your mind and re-centre. A strategy shared at the end of this chapter will help you to do this.

You can also use this time to review your activities and goals.

Common emotions: anger, frustration, stress, guilt, insecurity, doubt and a tendency to beat yourself up. Counteract these emotions with self-acceptance, self-love and self-care.

Hormonally: your oestrogen and progesterone levels begin low, leaving you feeling flat. Oestrogen gradually begins to build toward the end of the week which will lift your outlook. Progesterone drops subtly before building again.

Spring: Days 8-14

The dynamic phase of your cycle is when you get the most done. It is a productive and rewarding time of the month. Tasks left undone last week will be knocked out of the park this week. The goals you dreamed up last week are put into action. Your memory, thinking and ability to absorb and recall information is more acute.

Your need for sleep lessens and this is the time in your cycle you will feel most energetic. Late nights and early mornings are normal and unlike in other phases of your month, you won't feel lethargic as a result of reduced sleep.

Your sense of self-confidence and self-belief is at its highest. This is the time of the month where you want to socialise, connect and network. You won't be open to big, deep and meaningful conversations, you'll just want to have fun!

With your focus on making the most of your time, you can be seen as unempathetic. It's not that you don't care; rather this phase means you just want to enjoy your life.

In terms of personal development and mindset, this is the ideal time to use positive affirmations to inspire and motivate. Remember the repeating BS stories you tell yourself and the negative emotions assigned to them? Replacing these BS stories with repetitive positive affirmations at this time will build positive connections with emotions such as self-assuredness, confidence, trust and faith in yourself. At this time of the month you completely believe it. Be warned: Your enthusiasm for your goals can mean that instead of using a short, punchy affirmation, you may be tempted to create an affirmation for every goal you desire. Avoid doing this. Choose a handful of affirmations that sum up the overall desired outcome and you'll find the new stories will be more likely to stick.

Common emotions: happiness, joy, contentment, confidence, belief, cockiness, sexiness. Be mindful of others' emotional states. You're not as naturally supportive of them when you're feeling so great. Frustration can crop up when others aren't keeping up with you or if you get bored or impatient.

Hormones: your most feminine hormone, oestrogen, rapidly increases, preparing for ovulation in summer, resulting in you feeling more positive, upbeat and chattier. Progesterone gradually builds again, not yet hitting its peak. Towards the end of this week, testosterone will hit its monthly peak, potentially causing you to be more impulsive, daring and competitive, plus prompting a sharp spike in your libido with stronger and easier-to-achieve orgasms.

Summer: Days 15-21

The expressive phase of summer can be difficult to identify as it is a feeling phase, like the creative phase of autumn, although you feel positive emotions linked to who you are, connection and relationships.

Your personal goals become less important, as feeling and experiencing all the world offers and the people around you take priority. Patience, acceptance and listening become strengths during summer. You're less sensitive to criticism while more compassionate and understanding to those around you. Essentially, you have the inner emotional strength with the external care to express who you are authentically while helping and assisting others with your abilities.

Use this time to learn what those around you think and feel about common projects, your services and to strengthen relationships, as you will be a better communicator in the summer phase. It is the perfect time to encourage, guide, persuade and influence.

Common emotions: love, connection, empathy, support, fun, celebration, gratitude and appreciation. Pre-PMS symptoms can occur. Be mindful of saying yes too much and taking on more than you can handle. Guilt can also occur if you feel you are not doing enough to help others.

Hormones: oestrogen and testosterone drop for the first half of the week before oestrogen gently rises again. This means the first part of the week is a 'pre-PMS' time where you'll experience less intense symptoms of PMS, while the gentle rise mid-week levels out those pre-PMS symptoms. Progesterone slowly rises this week for its monthly peak, gradually sedating you, making you feel sleepy and foggy with a lower libido. Increased progesterone can cause you to feel blue.

Autumn: Days 22-28

This is your creative phase, the time of the month that can be the most challenging, as it can be unpredictable, changing from month to month. You can experience an overall gradual decline in stamina and positivity, or it can occur in sudden bursts. Autumn can be experienced as a wild ride of emotions with mental concentration and action as well as sensitivity and aggression. Structured and systematic thinking can be challenging, however you'll be more in tune with your intuition, so listen up!

Meditation becomes a natural state, as does tuning into your subconscious. Use this time proactively by asking yourself specific questions about what you want to experience in your life. Use strategic 'what' questions, then allow time for your subconscious mind to provide you with answers and inspired ideas. Combine this with time to daydream and visualise about what you desire then write it all down.

Avoid using positive affirmations though. In autumn, the BS you've stored deep within your subconscious will provide you with all the reasons, excuses, memories and nonsense to prove the positive affirmation is false (this is precisely why women need to use the Female Factor when working with personal development. Do the right thing for you at the right time of your cycle and you can create great transformation. Try to force the process according to the masculine, linear way of living and you could set yourself up for a fall).

Look inward and uncover what is really going on. Use the tracking sheet from Chapter 3 with "What am I doing? What am I thinking? What am I feeling?" to gain insight into the source and reasoning of your BS. Remember, these stories are simply that: stories and BS! Avoid exploring them any deeper other than to create awareness and proactive choices for change. Do not use 'why' questions, otherwise you'll find yourself spinning in circles and repeating the story over and over again.

Common emotions: mood swings with irritability, intolerance, guilt, sensitivity, drama queen moments, aggression, anxiety, creativity, communicating from the heart.

Hormones: oestrogen and progesterone take a dive. As oestrogen drops, moodiness, sadness, irritability, muscle aches, insomnia, headaches, fatigue and other PMS symptoms can show. You may start to feel more energetic because the progesterone that caused you to feel drowsy last week has dropped, clearing your head.

Now that you have some of the characteristics of each phase within your cycle, it's time to do something with it all and increase your personal power by better understanding YOU.

Start tracking what your cycle means for you. To accompany this book, you can find free resources at http://tinyurl.com/oybs-downloads The tracking sheet I included for you in this instance is set out on one single page, with the days of the month running across the top.

If you have a regular period, you probably have a fairly clear idea of what phase you are in now. Be open to tracking all these characteristics anyway as you will learn so much about yourself when you look for the different ways a phase impacts your life.

If you have no idea when your period starts (or if you don't have a period) simply start on today's date and make a mark for all symptoms which make sense for you. I included the most common indicators of a phase for you, however you can include your bathroom habits, specific headspace/emotional moods that are common for you along with thoughts and lines of thinking.

After a couple of months of tracking, you will start to work out when each phase comes and goes for you. I personally connect the dots across the pages so I have a visual clue on the rise and fall between my symptoms. With this, you can make a fairly educated guess of which phase is represented by which symptom. In the example below it's fairly likely that spring, the dynamic phase, is around the beginning of the month with winter, the reflective phase, towards the end.

Day		1	2	3	4	5	6	7	8	9	10	11	12	13	14	15	16	17	18	19	20	21	22	23	24	25	26	27	28	29	30	31
Emotional State	Happy	x	x	X	x	x																										
	Flat						x	X						x				x	x	x	x	x										
	Anxious												x		x								x	x	x	x				x	x	x
	Angry								x	x	x	x				x	x										x	x	x			

How does knowing this make a difference to you, the BS you get caught up in, and taking back your personal power?

Prior to knowing this, I spent a number of years on the Mirena IUD, with no period in between. I had no clue what phase I was in.

I started to explore more than my moods by tracking my sleep, thought processes and energy levels. Over time, I saw established highs and lows. My food cravings began to act as a giveaway for autumn; I crave chocolate and sugar just prior to my period starting. Once I saw these ebbs and flows, I began to analyse the overall theme of my moods and was surprised to see there was a pattern. For instance, I easily feel overwhelmed a few days before my winter. Everything becomes too much for me, I panic and have the habit of 'worst-case scenario' thinking.

Once I recognised this, I started to question where the emotion was coming from, was it controllable, was it justified, or was it just a 'thing' that happened?

I began to plan my activity to accommodate for my overwhelmed days, minimising expectations I had on myself, reducing my job list and recognising that if a situation was primed for me to feel overwhelmed, I had a choice regarding how heavily I invested myself in that situation.

I started to choose my battles with the kids more effectively during this time, creating space from them when I felt things were getting too much. I lowered my expectations of them and began to recognise that what really mattered for me at that time of the month was peace and love!

Just like being able to appreciate my husband's and son's brains for their naturally different ways, when I was able to allow my natural cycle and female way, I could further influence our family dynamics positively by not putting myself into a place of emotional vulnerability unnecessarily. I started having full ownership of me and my power.

This is what I hope the information about the Female Factor provides you with the opportunity to do.

Tip Time:

1. Download and print the tracking sheets accompanying this book, available free at: http://tinyurl.com/oybs-downloads During interactions with the men in your life, remember some of the differences between the way you process and the way they do. Share this with him so he too, can appreciate you and your female brain.
2. Learn to create, plan and live life according to your natural cycle. Regardless of the physical period you may or may not have, your cycle is more than menstruation. Everything from your thinking, sleeping, communication ability, eating, influencing others and energy levels is impacted by the fluctuations of your hormones. Learn to do the right things for you at the right times of your month and trust that the more you live your life in flow, the more productive, connected and empowered you will be.
3. Become a master of expanding your space. Try this exercise: find something to focus on right in front of you, slightly above your eye level. Consciously choose three things to the left of that point to become aware of. Find three things to the right. Notice the noises all around you. Take a deep breath. Feel the space you've created both in your mind and within your body. Take a number of deep breaths and enjoy this 'nothing' space that you have expanded.

CHAPTER 5

Rejecting the head talk and emotional baggage

If you look deeply into the palm of your hand, you will see your parents and all generations of your ancestors. All of them are alive in this moment. Each is present in your body. You are a continuation of each of these people

Thich Nhat Hanh

While studying the female brain in 2012, I was introduced to two incredibly powerful concepts that helped me to understand myself along with my family and friends in a whole new dimension. These two concepts helped me trust the process I was working through, giving me the confidence to share it with potential new clients. These two concepts are epigenetics and spiral dynamics. I'm going to give you a crash course in both of them during this chapter. This crash course, will hopefully provide you with a moment of clarity, the 'Aha!'

moment explaining some of your behavioural habits along with how you work and fit in with the people around you.

Prepare yourself though, it will get deep!

For years, it was believed who we are is a result of either nature (our genetic makeup) or nurture (our upbringing). Furthermore, our genetic makeup couldn't be changed, whatever we were given at birth was what we would have until the day we died. Science is now proving this is not necessarily the case, it's not black and white.

In his book *The Biology of Belief*, Bruce H Lipton PhD (2015 Hay House Australia Ltd), introduces readers to the transformation and change cells and genes can undertake when the right combination of events and hormones trigger a reaction, altering the behaviour of genes without changing the underlying DNA sequence. This is called epigenetics. The term epigenetics comes from the Greek prefix *epi*, meaning above or around, and 'genetics'.

It is how the change in gene expression affects how the cells read the genes.

Epigenetic change is a regular, natural occurrence and can be influenced by a number of factors, some of which we discuss in further detail. These factors include age, environment and lifestyle, hormonal fluctuations, events or a disease state. New and ongoing research continues to uncover details about the role of epigenetics. Scientifically speaking, genes are modified through one of three systems: DNA methylation, histone modification and non-coding RNS.

For the purpose of you being able to own your BS, we focus on behavioural epigenetics, the reasons why some of our emotions seem to 'come from nowhere' and take hold long term.

Let me break down this down.

Your body is made of up between 30–50 trillion cells. To put this in context, there are between 100–200 billion galaxies in the universe, which means you have around 800 million more cells within you than known galaxies in the universe!

Within every single cell lies the human genome, within which there are approximately 20,000 genes. Genes are segments of chromosomes which are made up of DNA and are important because they provide our cells with information on how to make proteins, which in layman terms means they make up the blueprint of who we are. Genes are made up of your family line, your parents, grandparents and great grandparents and form part of your genetic makeup.

DNA from one of your cells, if stretched out from one end to the other, would measure around 6 feet in length. If we connected all your DNA , strand to strand, the resulting strand would be 108 billion kilometres long or 150,000 round trips from Earth to the moon!

DNA is tightly bound around a group of proteins called histones, which essentially tell the genes how to behave. Histones can dictate your emotional state, beliefs and behaviour.

Now, I hear what you're thinking. "What the heck does all that mean and why are you telling me this, Bree?"

When I met my husband in 2002, I was a pretty easy going, happy, content woman. Aaron often comments that these qualities were one of the reasons he fell in love with me; I was adventurous, lots of fun and relaxed. Of course, I had my moments, I had doubts and insecurities, but they certainly didn't impact my life on a frequent enough basis for me to worry about them.

In late 2004, I began IVF medication to assist us in conceiving our son. For more than 18 months I had artificial hormone treatment on a monthly basis, which impacted my moods, making me harder to live with. We thought it was the hormone interference, but now we know my histones were also changing my natural demeanour. The combination of hormones and the stress, heartache and sadness accompanying the IVF journey of our lives was sapping my happiness and turning me negative.

We were blessed to conceive Blair in 2006, and with his birth in early 2007 things settled down again. The bliss of being a parent calmed my moods and headspace.

I fell pregnant with Alivia in 2008 and the moods came back. When she was born in 2009, things didn't really improve. We had added to the stress by moving cities and purchasing a house that needed serious renovations, so there was something already different about me as a person, however.

Aaron frequently said, "It's like you've changed – I just want the 'old' Bree back, the happy and carefree Bree." To which I would reply (scream) "DON'T YOU THINK I WANT THAT TOO? I CAN'T HELP IT!"

It felt like a switch had been flicked somewhere deep within me, and for the life of me I couldn't change it back. This was why when I was introduced to epigenetics and I started to understand how these switches worked, I trusted it and followed my gut.

Why did I go from being a happy, carefree woman to a screaming, crazy banshee? Within my genetic makeup lay over-the-top reactions, anger, guilt and embarrassment among other emotions. These traits had lain dormant within my genes until my hormones triggered the switch to flick on, thanks to the IVF medication.

My first pregnancy triggered a few more switches and my second pregnancy more.

When we moved to the 'Renovation House from Hell' in Newcastle, the stress activated more switches.

Slowly, the switches began to surface until "I just became a new, crazy Bree".

Remember earlier I mentioned there are a number of factors which can trigger the modifications of your genes? Two of the most significant factors for women are your hormones and an event.

As women, we experience a number of significant hormonal fluctuations throughout our lifetime.

Puberty sets it off; this is why so many young girls seem to go through a metamorphosis of both personality and mood. Anxiety, stress, anger, depression and insecurities seem to 'turn up overnight' which can sometimes be linked to the family as passed-on traits, that is to say, an epigenetic switch is activated.

Pregnancy can alter it with extreme fluctuations and changes to accommodate the growing of baby, which changes who you feel you are, resulting in previously unfelt emotions rearing women's heads.

Peri-menopause and menopause mean just when you think you have some traction on who you are and what your life means to you, another fluctuation of hormones kicks in, potentially altering your base mood all over again.

With events, when you think about all the events over the course of a lifetime, becoming a parent, professional roles, sudden and unexpected changes, death, severe illness, relationships changing and so on, it's no wonder you can feel like a 'switch just goes off', leaving you as a new or different version of you.

Look at my example of going from carefree to crazy. My switches flicked because of both an event (the move) and my hormones (my pregnancies). Since then, a handful of small events and one significant event have acted as the trigger for a significant emotional change in my personality.

Thankfully, I gained a conscious understanding of why the changes were happening, and as a result, I was able to work through it better than my original encounter with flicking switches!

The Family Cycle

The exploration of epigenetics has shown up to 7 generations of emotional baggage, beliefs and habits lay within your genes, stored on the histotags on our DNA. Tim Spector's book 'Identically Different: Why you can change your Genes, 2013 of Orion Books Ltd, the article Epigenetic Programming by Maternal Behaviour. M Meaney & M Szyf 2004 – Nature Neuroscience Journal and the 2012 TedTalk by Courtney Griffins, 'Epigenetics and the influence of our genes' are just a few examples of these studies being documented and explored.

How does that impact on your emotional state?

For many women, it is simple to recognise family traits. Maybe you suffer from an emotional state like anxiety. When you explore it, you see anxiety is present in your mum's life and an aunty, grandmother or other relatives (if you know the extended family history).

Maybe you relate to anger issues, when you explore your family line you see common struggles within your father's family.

You might recognise a family trait that is expressed in both your mother and father's line and is now evident in your own life, and if you have children, you may see this trait appear in their lives.

Even if you don't know much detail about the traits, baggage or experiences of previous generations in your family line, it is safe to assume there were females in your family before you who experienced circumstances and events which had them feeling doubt, uncertainty, stress, anxiety, anger, worthlessness, inequality, suppression, not being heard, unvalued etc. This is why the studies of epigenetics make incredible sense for women who are struggling with an emotion they don't fully understand.

Along with emotional traits, belief systems such as "I'm not good enough", "Money is hard to come by", "This is our lot in life" and "Life is hard"' are passed on, supporting why many family members follow in the steps of family before them.

I share this information about epigenetics not to blame our parents or ancestors. Their decisions were made based on the knowledge, resources, headspace and judgement they had available to them at the time. Just like you, your parents, grandparents, aunties, uncles, great grandparents (and beyond) did the best they could.

While we are not laying blame, we can understand why we have some of the traits, thoughts and emotions we do.

It's good to know a switch which can be flicked on to activate any emotion or belief can also be switched off. It can be changed or altered, possibly not to the state you were before. As every change allows for growth, however, it can lose its charge and allow you to regain a balanced view of your life.

CASE STUDY: Pauline, Mother of 2 Adults (My Mum!), Office Manager

As one of the eldest in a large family, Pauline remembers always feeling unworthy, not good enough and having low self-esteem, particularly when she compared herself to her siblings. Questioning and doubting her abilities and decisions was second nature, something that followed her from childhood through to adulthood. She felt she could never speak her mind, people walked all over her, and worse, she felt she let them because she didn't have the strength to stand up.

Pauline decided to take back her power when she recognised guilt from her past was dominating her life. She was fed up with not having confidence in herself, allowing others to dictate her life, knowing that she was allowing things to happen that she wasn't comfortable with but was too insecure to object to. Although her children were grown, she felt haunted by a belief she had let her children down.

Since owning her BS, Pauline learned not to beat herself up. She recognises she didn't have control over every situation that resulted in poor past choices and forgave herself regarding those decisions, knowing she was doing the best she could at the time. "I have a much better relationship with myself and the most important people in my life. I know that I am responsible for my own choices, just as the people around me are responsible for their own. I am more tolerant of my peers and recognise that it's not always about me – I don't need to internalise and take things personally. I am a much happier person and no longer carry guilt, self-doubt and unworthiness. I believe I am a good wholesome person who has a great deal to offer."

(This case study is such an honour to share with you! When I started to see the power and control available to women, the first person I wanted to 'help' was naturally my mum. I could see common family traits I shared with her and other members of our family. I knew the difference that was made and felt when all those heavy things were released. She needed to be ready to release all that wasn't serving her, though. It took almost 4 years until finally she was ready to let it all go, and boy was it worth it! My mum is a vibrant, confident and strong woman, one who now stands her ground and knows her worth. It's been a true blessing to share this gift with her.)

The second concept that altered my reality is spiral dynamics.

Spiral dynamics is a different way of seeing human nature. It's more than a personality test; it's the system of beliefs and values within an individual which triggers their behaviour. Originally identified by Dr Clare W Graves throughout the '50s and '60s then further explored and developed by two of his students, Christopher Cowen and Don Beck, who later wrote a book on their theory of the same name 'Spiral Dynamics – mastering values, leadership and change"(2011, Blackwell Publishing Ltd) . It creates a structure to better understand how individuals, organisations and societies think, respond and behave.

This theory is complex and can be explored in depth. However, I summarise the key points so you can see how knowing the way people in your life fit into the spiral can influence your world.

Essentially, spiral dynamics separates personal traits, levels of thinking and behaviour into a various number of zones, each characterised by a number of memes – values that identify and describe a person's nature. The zones fit on a spiral, indicating that in order to grow up a level, we must first move through the current or previous zone. Thus, at all times, we have traits from previous zones within us, some more dominant than others.

The traditional spiral is split into 8 zones and 2 tiers. The first tier starts with 5 zones, each being identified with a colour: beige, purple, red, blue, orange and green. The second tier offers the yellow and turquoise zones and generally make up less than 2% of the population. Here, I'll introduce you to tier 1 only.

Specific qualities are identified in each zone and while people will identify with various aspects of many zones, there will be one zone which feels dominant, and therefore can be assumed as the zone where that particular person is currently sitting. Like any model of personal development, with awareness and lessons, people grow from one zone into another.

The more you can identify characteristics of those around you, the more you can empathise, motivate and understand them, providing you with the opportunity to create strong connections with many people from different backgrounds. It gives you a different insight into yourself and how other people fit into your picture of your world, and vice versa.

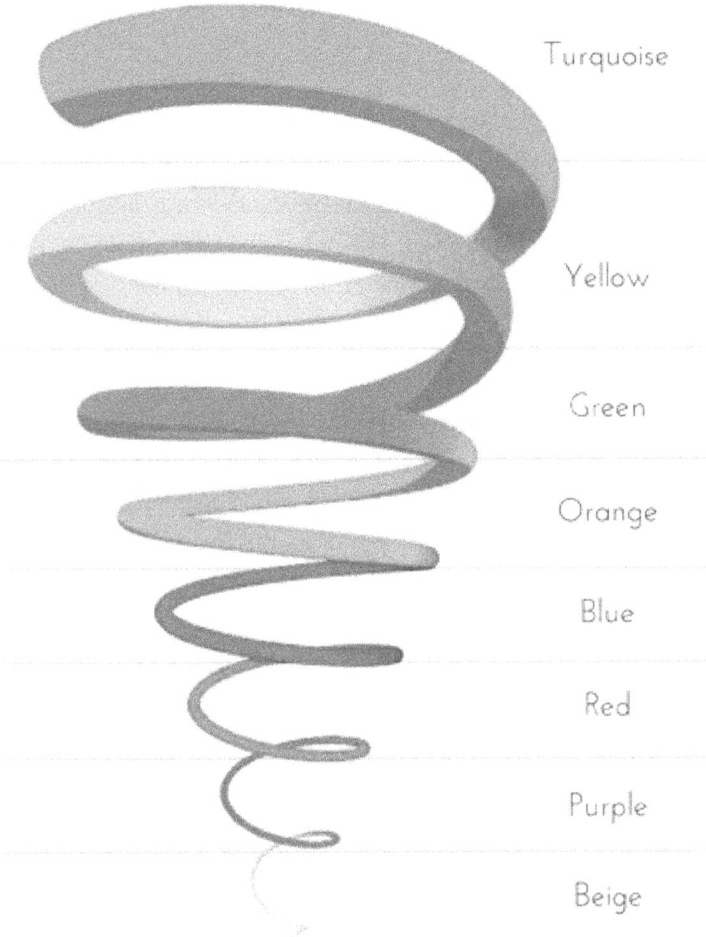

Zone one, at the bottom of the spiral, is beige and is represented by a 'survival' mentality. The focus of those in Beige centres around where they are going to sleep, eat and how they will get through day to day. They have little awareness of those outside of themselves and is typically represented by a newborn baby or the homeless. As a result, a minority of modern civilisation is in the zone of beige.

Zone two is the purple zone, characterised by tribal thinking, the stories of myths and legends. They believe in mystical, sacred objects, places and events with a strong allegiance to a chief, elders, ancestors or tribal leaders. Modern-day purple can be found in tarot readers and fortune tellers, taking their cues from signs around them. Approximately 10% of the adult population strongly relates to the purple zone.

Zone three is the red zone which 20-30% of the population can be characterised by. It's recognised by a strong sense of loyalty and determination. Those in the red zone can be considered selfish, with a strong motivation to please and serve self. They have high expectations of those around them, with little appreciation in return. They demand attention and respect, rarely feel guilt, lack empathy for others, can be quick to anger and accuse others for their emotional reactions.

Women I work with often have people in the red zone as triggers in their lives. These dominant personalities lead women to question themselves or second guess their dreams, desires and actions. I encourage my clients who identify 'red' people in their lives to pick their battles wisely. Arguing with a red is generally pointless, as, unless they are growing through and out of the dominant red zone, they will rarely acknowledge or be open to others' opinions.

Reds have an extremely strong sense of loyalty, particularly towards family and friends, along with a strong sense of strength, self-preservation and persistence.

Zone four is the blue zone with the majority of the population residing here, 30-40% in fact. Those in the blue zone love stability, systems and steps. They thrive on knowing there is structure, a clear set of expectations and guidelines. Blue people in our community established and sustain the order we have. With a strong sense of 'wanting to belong', feeling safe and secure, they will do just about anything to avoid punishment. Those in the blue zone are often anxious, prone to stress and guilt. People who identify with the blue zone are traditional, preferring the 'known' over the 'new', needing multiple facts and backing in order to accept a new way of thinking. The code of conduct many blue people live by is truth, honesty and respect.

In the 'real world' we see blue in the education and medical systems, religious houses and long-established organisations and corporations. They have a 'rule book' which sets out the steps, expectations and potential outcomes.

Growing from blue, we move into the fourth zone or orange zone, characterised by a sense to improve the system, found in 20-30% of the adult population. Many CEOs, business executives, entrepreneurs and professionals with a seat of power are in the orange zone. Personal achievement, materialistic gain, reputation, pride and success tend to be driving forces for those in the orange zone. While competition is strong within the orange world, it allows for expertise to blossom.

Comparison is a trap some experience in the orange zone. Comparing oneself to another allows insecurity and doubt to arise.

The fifth and final zone of the first tier is the green zone, which has an emphasis on sharing, networking, collaborating and connecting. Creating relationships, strengthening personal development and values has a high focus. Spirituality is refreshed to bring harmony and enrich the living experience. In green, people begin to recognise the necessity of all the different zones, although they struggle to completely accept each level for its own individual strengths and weaknesses.

Characteristics of the green zone include a desire for inner peace, personal strength and equal opportunity for all. Emotions are often accepted, allowed and processed healthily, although a fear of rejection and disapproval from the world around them can remain.

What's the point of introducing you to all of this? Particularly, when the purpose of this book is to help you own your BS?

Many of the stories, thoughts and memories you tell yourself on a regular basis are connected to other people, right?

When you had arguments with your loved ones in the past, you were probably been left asking questions like:

"Why do they keep doing that?", "Why can't we see eye to eye?" or "Why can't they just see my point of view?" Then you felt guilty, angry, not good enough and ashamed. This often comes down to not understanding each other and these questions further add to the BS you're telling yourself.

When you work towards a professional goal, if you start to compare yourself to another woman, you begin to question your ability, capability and skill because you aren't fully understanding what drives and motivates her, or yourself.

If you are a woman of influence and you're trying to encourage a team member, employee or client to grow, yet you 'just can't seem to reach them', you might be using the wrong driving force or priorities to truly reach her.

What would happen if you could first identify then become truly comfortable with where you currently sit on the spiral?

Understanding, self-compassion, insight into how you are inspired, what drives your emotions, thoughts and beliefs will all be identified and explored. You can see where in your life you can improve and grow, where your limitations are and where your strengths are. What happens when you have this insight into yourself? Self-confidence has the opportunity to grow!

What would happen if you were able to identify where those people in your world were on the spiral?

If you identified red zone people, who, despite how much they love you, are probably always going to have limited understanding and openness to your opinions while they are in the red zone, you save yourself some grief and pick your battles wisely. Stand down when it doesn't really matter and shut off their opinions, knowing it does not have anything do with you and everything to do with them.

If you identified the blues in your life, who love tradition, rules and the known, you might limit the conversations of 'big deep ideas' with them, knowing that although they believe in and support you, they just don't understand anything outside of convention as it's simply not in their current belief system.

Owning your BS is as much about knowing and recognising what your BS is, as it is knowing what BS other people are trying to feed you. When you know what they value, what their thinking habits and beliefs are, you will be capable of leave their BS to them!

As my client Magali said when we started thinking about the impact knowing this information had in her life (as a mother, management executive and entrepreneur), *"It helped me realise we are all at different levels of 'being' human – it helps explain why people react and behave in certain ways and why they are reacting or interacting with us the way they do. Therefore, it really is ok for me to be detached in my relations and reactions with them, because it is not about me, but them. As such, I do not need to try and change myself to please others, nor do I need to beat myself up about what I have said to them, or about their judgements of me. I can just keep doing what I believe is best for me (and my family)."*

Tip Time:

1. To continue the journey of owning your BS with this new information, start to identify what your habits are.
   Ask yourself:
   What beliefs do you have just because?
   What are your thinking habits? Do your emotional reactions that weigh you down?
   What family traits can you identify with that play a significant part of who you are today, and what can you do to learn from this realisation?
   How do these habits affect you?

2. Identify peers and family members who can help develop your awareness of these habits. What can you learn from these people? How can they teach and influence you to move forward?
   Begin to create a picture of where the people in your life sit on the spiral. Do their values and beliefs align with yours? How can you alter your interactions with the people on the spiral who cause you conflict? How can you take back your power with these people? How can you try to teach and influence those around you?

3. Start to take ownership of how the relationships and habits in your life impact your day-to-day reality. What can you do to streamline and simplify things? Where can you make adjustments? Where can you detach from the habits that don't serve you?
   What new habits can you start to create?
   For the people in your life who cause you discomfort, how can you prepare yourself for interactions with them? For example, when I know I am spending time with 'red' people, I'm mindful to deflect their opinions if they don't align with mine and remind myself not to take it personally when we disagree on topics.

CHAPTER 6

Transformations to create the new you

Clarity comes from knowing what you want and from moving in the direction of it. Your soul is guiding and supporting you every step of the way!

- Sue Krebs

Groundhog Day.

Living life on a merry-go-round.

Cycling a round-a-bout.

Feeling like every new day is a repeat of the day before.

For many women, life has become a repetitious experience that promotes doing what needs to be done, instead of creating a life that is actually desired.

January turns into June in the blink of an eye and before you know it, it's Christmas time and the start of a new year approaches.

"This year will be different!" you think to yourself every January 1. "I'm going to get fit, I'm going to be successful, I'm going to be a better mum."

Then it's June again and nothing changed.

Over the past few years, I have noticed more women are describing their lives as lost, stuck or lacking direction. It's my belief this is happening because we lost sight of what we actually want and enjoy from life. Instead, we focus on problems we perceive ourselves to be experiencing or we spend our time doing what we think we need to be doing, not what actually lights us up. We live our daily lives following unspoken expectations! It is worse is when it's a combination of focusing on problems and following expectations. It creates a huge mess!

Problem focus, as we established in prior chapters, increases negative emotions felt in the body and limits perceived opportunities all around. Levels of doubt are increased as we become confused about what we want, confused about why we want these things, then completely stuck on how to make any of it happen.

Living according to unspoken expectations results in feeling insecure, doubtful and incompetent.

This adds to the thoughts and stories of the past, which are already mixed up in our extremely busy heads!

It's no wonder women feel lost, stuck and lacking direction!

This chapter is dedicated to identifying what is most important in your life. To bring some zest, direction and clarity back!

In years leading up to owning my BS, I put everything I thought was important to me as a priority – being successful and positive all the time, looking the part and creating a heap of materialistic representations of 'perfection'. Seeming like a tender mum who loved every last bit of motherhood.

I lived my life thinking it was unacceptable to show negative emotion and voice my struggles. To be successful, I could not share my troubles. I was to create an image other women could look up to, that looked 'perfect' on the surface regardless of the bubbling underneath. I firmly held the belief that if I admitted how much I actually struggled in the role of being a mum, I was then undeserving of being a mum because it was wrong to think anything other than "this is the best".

IT WAS SO MUCH PRESSURE!

Looking back at the mess I created, it's no wonder I struggled with all those masks every time I acted 'outside of perfect'. I felt guilty, like a fraud, not ready to be successful or professional and all the rest of it.

As I started to work through the BS stories I was telling myself, I began focusing on what was really important. The things I valued in my life, which I lacked because I was no longer making them a priority, became a priority again. The clearer I became on what was really important, the more I recognised how unnecessary the rest of the BS was. I stopped being trapped, living life according to an expectation or belief that held me back. Instead, I was able to make decisions which served my greater good and allowed alignment and harmony to come back into my life.

That's what we're going to do for you. In the time I've worked with women, one thing consistently comes up which fuels conflict and inner turmoil: a misalignment with what is most important to each individual woman's life. When a woman is investing her time and energy in things which don't support who she is at her core, which is represented by what she values, she feels discomfort. Discomfort shows itself in negative emotion and behaviour.

What is a value? Why is it so important to know what you value in your life?

Your initial thoughts might turn to characteristics such as love, respect, loyalty, honesty or integrity. It's no surprise if this is the case, as people who have done any kind of value work have been taught to know what these 'qualities' of values are.

In order to best represent who we are, we need to know which characteristics we value, what we are looking for in the relationships around us, the jobs we take, clients we work with and so on. We need to know what these characteristics are so we can raise our children with these values as a foundation for them to build on. When we know these characteristics, it enables us to avoid people and situations which cause conflict with what we value in other people.

In order for us to begin creating a life with direction, we need to know more than characteristics. We need to become aware of the people we value, relationships we cherish, experiences we appreciate and experiences we want more of in life – the elements of life that make us feel safe and protected yet strong and capable. Consider these values your Inspiration Motivators.

In order to create harmony in all aspects of life, it's good to know what is important to you in every aspect of your life. A harmonious life is created when there is equilibrium between all facets of life, a gentle tug and pull between priorities to keep things in alignment. If you feel unbalanced, it's possibly because you've given one part of your life more priority than others, which results in this part taking up more time and attention than necessary.

Let's look at what your Inspiration Motivators are and create clarity around what you want so you can create balance.

Start with you as an individual. What is important to you? Your personal development, happiness, soul/spirit connection, faith, health and fitness. Nine times out of 10 when I do this exercise with women, they don't consider themselves as something which needs to be important in their lives! Beliefs such as "It's selfish to put me first" cause this, however it couldn't be further from the truth! Let me give you a reality check:

You are in the mess of BS, emotional fog, confusion, feeling lost and stuck, without direction and clarity around your life because you've put everyone else ahead of your own life for too long!

Chances are, you literally lost yourself in everyone else's needs. It is a common scenario, particularly for mums, because so much of our time is devoted to the upbringing and wellness of children. Professional women can relate this to the new, formative years of a business or career. Your time and energy goes into something or someone outside of you. As your children, career and business mature, their needs change, maybe things become more automated, independence is gained, the demands on your personal time alter, yet you continue to put them first. The end result? Your current situation!

Ask yourself, "What is important to me as an individual, outside of other people?"

What relationships are important to you? Review your romantic partnership, children, family, both close and extended, friendships, professional relationships and any relationship which adds to your experience of life. How does the web of your relationships intersect? How does it look to you? How does it feel when you give these relationships the recognition they deserve?

An earth-shattering realisation came for me when I truly recognised, emotionally and intellectually, how important my family is to me. For too long, I put my business and professional image above my family. This happened due to my struggles within myself of being a mum. I rarely allowed myself to acknowledge how important Aaron and our kids were to me. I almost felt like it was a given, which in turn prevented me from really appreciating them. The moment I recognised, felt and acknowledged my family as a priority to me, the drive behind my business completely shifted. My world became clearer – my purpose, motivation and inspiration for everything else in my life, my professional success and personal development felt incredibly easier once I knew it was all because of them. Everything I did, everything I do now, is because of the life I'm creating with my family.

As a woman, it's incredibly important to honour the relationships which are important to us; to give them the time, space and acknowledgement that complete our experiences. All the rest of the BS, the challenges, lessons and tribulations fade away in comparison to the connections we make with people who are important to us. So, what relationships are important to you? What connections do you want to nurture properly?

What is important to you professionally? Is it a career? Advancement? Being self-employed or having the security of a specific role in a great organisation? Learning and challenging yourself? Influencing others? What do you want to achieve, for you? Being a leader or a great team player? What do you want from yourself professionally? What do you want this to allow for you, your family and your friends?

What is important to you within the world? Travelling, education, experiencing and learning from different cultures and beliefs? What experiences do you want in your life? What experiences do you want for yourself, and what do you want to share with people who are important to you? What do you want to see and enjoy?

When you identify the different things in your life that hold value for you, you begin to make decisions that support what's important to you and they become all the Inspiration Motivators you need! Confusion lessens; the fog begins to clear. Even better, you're less likely to make decisions and put yourself into situations that conflict with what is important to you. You won't consciously choose to compromise what makes you happy.

Take some time now. Look into your soul and ask yourself: What is important to you?

Read through the above questions and examples then allow yourself to recognise everything that is important to you. Write it down. Don't try to make logical sense of anything or order and prioritise the list. Simply put it all on paper, then come back to me when you are done!

I have included a template that you are welcome to download and print http://tinyurl.com/oybs-downloads

How does it feel, seeing the list of people, things and dreams that are important to you? What happens within your body as you acknowledge those things? It's good, isn't it? It feels powerful to acknowledge what is important to you!

I am aware a list of this depth can be confronting for some, particularly if you recognised not every item on the list is being fulfilled. Overwhelm can creep up, so we're going to simplify things for you.

Start by getting a reality check on your current situation. Move through the list you've written and give each item a score of satisfaction between 0 and 10, with 0 being 'man that needs some serious work' and 10 being 'I can't see how this could get any better'. Once you've completed it, date your piece of paper so, in the future you can track how things have improved (and on the other side, if you begin to feel unsettled again in the future, look over this list and identify where your satisfaction scores have slipped, which will give you an opportunity to make amendments).

This entire list represents everything important to you. In the act of providing you with direction and clarity, of inspiring you for action, we're going to identify what holds the highest priority for you right now. Like everything in life, these priorities may shift and change over time, and that's good; it's evolution and growth. We want to focus on working out your highest priorities right now by identifying 3 top priorities. Keeping your focus on 3 things at a time allows for more clarity and less confusion or overwhelm.

Let's work out what your heart desires most from this list. You'll need to get out of your head because it's been conditioned to approach everything from the logical and sensible angle, which is not respecting your Female Factor! So, lets tap into your heart space, your intuition… into you!

Step 1. Look at the first item on your list. Feel what this feels like for you. Allow it to settle in your body for a moment.

Step 2. Now look at the second item and feel it.

Step 3. When you compare the two, which one feels, in your heart and gut, that it has more pull, intensity and importance? Choose one.

Step 4. Compare this chosen item with the next item on your list by repeating Steps 1, 2 & 3.

Work through your list in this manner until you identify the one item on the list which holds the most emotional pull and importance for you. Put a big 1 next to it.

Step 5. Repeat the entire process again to identify your number 2 and number 3.

Good work! Now you know what your current top 3 priorities are.

Sit back and admire that for a moment.

How does it feel? What would happen in your life if every decision you made supported these three things? How much simpler will your decision-making process become? Trust me, it's an extremely powerful acknowledgement to have!

CASE STUDY: Caren - De Facto Relationship,

Mother of 2 Adult Children, Respite Support Nurse And Budding Entrepreneur

Prior to owning her BS, Caren was an extremely insecure woman, lacking self-confidence and self-belief. She'd been working as a respite worker for many years, primarily because Caren loved to help people. With her natural gift for connecting to other people, her tenderness made for a beautiful support person in challenging environments. Deep down though, Caren had a desire to change professional direction, to go out on her own and follow a different passion. Her limiting beliefs prevented her from having the courage to make things happen.

As a result, Caren often felt angry with herself, with the limitations she couldn't see past such as prior education and her current age. As a mature woman, she often found herself thinking, "I can't do this, I'm too old, I'm not smart enough, witty enough, quick enough to make it happen". Every dream and idea Caren had was quickly shut down with a loud inner voice telling her, "You can't!"

Being caught up in this negative head talk left Caren exhausted and emotionally drained. Regardless of the effort she applied, she wasn't living up to her potential. She compared herself to peers, friends and other professionals, always seeing herself as 'less than'. After identifying and addressing her BS, Caren is now pursuing a new career! "I know that there is no need to compare myself with other women, that ultimately I am enough, I am likeable and loveable – even better, I love myself for who I am. Now that I've been able to honour my BS, I feel so much better about what I'm capable of – there is almost no negative head talk anymore, and when something does come up, I'm able to rely on a strategy to gain clearer perspective again. I rarely stress. I'm so much more connected to me, to my dreams and to my family. Knowing what is important to me has given me the confidence to follow my heart, to make decisions that support my life and also encourage my two grown children to do the same, to chase their dreams, to push past limitations and create new beliefs for themselves, because it really is ok to take baby steps and to do things at your own pace, in your own way. Owning my BS has improved my life and the life of my family in ways I never imagined."

Let's take those Inspiration Motivators even deeper now!

Knowing what's most important to you is the first level of personal power. Now, we are going to explore your top 3 values in depth.

On a new piece of paper (or go to http://tinyurl.com/oybs-downloads where I created a template for you) and write down your Number 1 value at the top of the page.

Underneath it, write the following question:

Why is that important to me?

Quiet your mind and ask yourself that one question again and again. List everything that comes to mind. When your thoughts slow down, ask it again, "Why is that important to me?" Push past the discomfort that may rise. Keep asking and exploring this question until you feel you have emptied your thoughts and feelings.

What you are identifying now are the beliefs (and sometimes the BS!) you keep telling yourself that either support or sabotage what you value. It is a big lightbulb moment for many women. Allow the process to take however long it needs to take. If you become emotional, acknowledge what you feel (you could use your awareness tracking sheet from the free downloads http://tinyurl.com/oybs-downloads), so you can claim more ownership around it. Remember it is ok to feel!

A belief is traditionally a statement a person holds true about a particular thing or event. If the belief is negative and doesn't support your value, chances are you are struggling to experience your value in its greatest capacity.

Say you value financial security. When you explore that, you come up with "Because without financial security I'm not safe, I'm struggling to pay bills and provide for my family" or "Because my parents always struggled financially and I don't want that for my life".

Or, say you value health and fitness "Because you don't want to be fat", "Because you don't want to die young", "Because you won't attract a partner unless you're buff."

Both beliefs are examples of belief systems which do not support the desire for financial security or health. It doesn't mean your beliefs are wrong. However, if they are not serving you and the life you want for yourself, are they beliefs you want to continue to hold on to?

If beliefs of a similar nature come up and you want to neutralise the negative intensity, use the Red Flag/White Word exercise from Chapter 3 to rewrite your belief consciously. Remember, you need to acknowledge whatever emotion comes up, feel it, then work through it.

It is confronting to see what you believe around what you want. That's ok, though. Acknowledgement is the first step to ownership. This is your journey; it takes time and you are well on your way to further explore your mind!

After identifying what you believe, create an action plan; a proactive list of things you can do to further support or increase how your top 3 values are showing up for you in your life. Determine 3 actionable steps you can take for each value on a regular basis.

For example, say you identified building your career is important to you, it inspires and motivates you. Now you know what you believe about that, having used the Red Flag/ White Word exercise, you can neutralise the negative and pick up positive beliefs. What can you do to continue to support your career right now? Maybe its enrol in that course you keep putting off, create a habit of leaving your work at work so you can restore balance between work and your family or become aware of what your strengths are within your current role, to make a list and read every day.

If your family is a current Inspiration Motivator, you can start to assign a day once a month for device-free family day or a regular games night at home with hubby to encourage reconnection or compile a list of things you appreciate about each member of your family and keep it somewhere handy so you can read it whenever you feel frustrated, agitated or upset with them.

I personally love this "to do list" because when you prioritise it and implement even one activity a day, you are taking an active step toward creating what you want from your life! You take back your power!

Committing to Change

It's all well and good to know what is important to you now. What if during this process, you identify some things that need altering and adjusting? How do you keep this newfound conviction strong? Just like owning your BS, it requires commitment from you.

Ask yourself the following:

- Am I completely committed to improving my life? How will my life improve when I implement these alterations? Who else is going to benefit? What will happen if I don't commit to improving my life? Am I prepared for that outcome?
- Am I prepared to commit to the commitment, to push through the challenges that rise knowing the end result is going to be worth it? Am I ready to give up blame (excuses), take responsibility and do what I can to make it happen? How is that going to improve my life when I commit to it?
- Am I ready to give it my all and not be mistaken with aiming for perfection, but rather to give it my best effort every day, learn from the slip ups and keep pushing on when necessary?
- Am I prepared to listen to my gut and make changes my gut tells me I need to follow through with?

Remember, you aren't changing you; you aren't voiding your past, you are simply allowing for transformations to take place that will create the life you desire.

NB: Beliefs (like emotional blocks) are often so deeply ingrained that doing a simple activity like the Red Flag/White Word exercise isn't going to magically replace a belief you've had for a long time. Deep transformation is often required and working with a coach or expert will often help you recreate beliefs for a long-term result.

Creating awareness and connection to your desire to change or adjust the belief is a great first step, and if you use positive affirmations at the appropriate time of your cycle, you will encourage these new beliefs to be heard and absorbed by your unconscious mind.

It's a deep insight to who you are, who you want to be, what you stand for and what you want, isn't it? Doesn't it feel powerful to focus on what you love and what is important to you, rather than the stories, problems and BS which previously dominated your thinking?

Become comfortable with listening to your gut, looking for how your actions are in alignment with what's important to you or how they are out of alignment. Be ok with making adjustments as needed, remembering everything you do has the potential to sabotage or support, destroy or create, remove or increase power.

Tip Time

When things feel unsettled or in conflict, chances are something in your life is out of alignment. Revisit what is most important to you frequently.

1. Start with a blank piece of paper (or download your templates http://tinyurl.com/oybs-downloads. What is important to you as an individual? What is important to you professionally? What relationships are important to you? What in the world is important to you?

2. Rate your current level of satisfaction within this list. Items with a low score might require more attention (or, if the current low satisfaction doesn't trouble you, take that as a sign this is how it's meant to be right now. Maybe this item doesn't need your attention right now!)

3. With your heart and gut, identify what your 3 current priorities are.

4. Ask yourself: Why is this important to me? If there is some negative belief that doesn't support your value, remember to neutralise it with the last chapter's tips and the Red Flag/White Word exercise.

5. Create a proactive list of activities you can do to support, increase and improve how these 3 values are showing up in your life.

6. When you are faced with a decision, remember your proactive list; work out all options available to you with this decision. Which choice supports and aligns with your list of values most? Where are the compromises, and are you ok with them? As you make decisions based on what is important to you and your direction, happiness and clarity will continue to unfold.

CHAPTER 7

Smart Heart goals

Determine what you want and why you want it.
Once you understand what's important,
you can utilize your passions and achieve anything!

Brooke Griffin

From 2010 to 2011, my husband and I renovated an old house on an incredibly tight budget. It was probably one of the most desperate situations we experienced as a couple.

We were emotionally drained, the kids were challenging, and at the time Alivia was an atrocious sleeper. A 3-hour stint was a marathon for her! Symptoms of Blair's ADHD were beginning to really show themselves; he was bouncing off the walls all day, every day. My attitudes and behaviours were escalating, my poor husband had it coming from all three of us, and to top it off, our physical environment was not safe and sound.

Financially, we were stretched, in debt up to our eyeballs with minimal income, while trying to renovate a house with major problems. For 12 weeks, electricity was in one room only. There were holes in the floors and walls because we didn't have the money to put proper coverings on them. We relied on cardboard and duct tape to keep the bugs out. When we thought it couldn't get any worse, the kitchen literally rotted out underneath the sink and benches! It took 5 months before we could afford a replacement kitchen.

We felt trapped in a situation we couldn't see a way out of. Aaron was working 6 days a week, renovating of an evening and weekend to try and make the house at least appear like a home.

Not long after the kitchen fell apart, I went to a Leader Development Day my company was running. They talked about setting a SMART goal (Specific, Measurable, Attainable, Realistic and Timely) and how to use the obstacles in your life as the fuel of motivation. I sat in the class and thought, "Well hell, Bree, you have no kitchen, there are holes in your floors and you are struggling BIG time! By the definition of obstacles, I'd say you have plenty of reasons to get off your ass!"

I worked out my SMART goal. I knew how much money I needed to make for a new kitchen and when I wanted it by. I worked out what activity was required to make that money. I worked out how to fit that activity into my diary. I had everything I needed to make this goal a reality. It was a SMART goal. Therefore, based on what I'd been taught, it was sure to be a success, right?

Nope. Even though I had every logical reason to push through and make it happen (we had no kitchen!) I initially struggled to get out of my own way.

Why?

My story is not uncommon. During my time working with women, I would say 90% of women who set a goal fall short and quit before they achieve it. It doesn't matter what kind of goal it is: a professional goal to promote themselves and increase their income, a personal goal such as get fit, attract a new partner, strengthen a relationship or financial goal such as save for the dream holiday. Motivation and inspiration quickly disappear.

You can invest hundreds, sometimes thousands of dollars to attend a conference or seminar in the hope you find inspiration to achieve what you want in your life and that they will have the answer you've been searching for all these years.

You leave feeling absolutely pumped, more excited, motivated and enthusiastic than you ever have in the past. This is it: the change you wanted in your life is just around the corner. The goal, achievement, relationship and life you want is at your fingertips! You can see the light at the end of the tunnel, because this event you went to has changed your life.

You invest hours following the formula the experts taught you.

A month into the journey you hit a hiccup. "Maybe I can't do this. I've never managed to follow through with something like this before." Your natural levels of motivation decreased because of your Female Factor, something not included in the SMART formula! You start to beat yourself up.

Your motivation takes a dive.

Then you remember the experts telling you, "It will be worth it. Push through the discomfort and keep your eyes focused on the end result." Your hormone levels change, you start to feel more positive and for a while, you remain motivated, although the belief you have in yourself is slowly losing its power.

Life gets in the way again. Old stories of "I can't do this!" and "I'll never be good enough!" start again, louder than before. Maybe they coincide with the autumn or winter part of your cycle and you remember all the times you've previously tried and failed.

The SMART goal no longer holds real emotional power within you.

It slips away into the 'one day' or 'maybe' pile with all the other unreached goals and achievements you've wanted in your life.

Or maybe you are the coach, the one sharing strategies, insights and inspiration to your team, clients and family members. You can see the person you want to help lose confidence, faith and motivation in what they wanted for themselves. You can't help but question why your methods don't work long term for the women you work with. It feels like there is something missing.

We are all familiar with this pattern, either from our own experiences or from the outside, observing it in others.

How the hell do we break that? How do we ensure what's been taught in this book doesn't slip into the 'that book I read once' pile?

How did I get my motivation back so I not only paid for a new kitchen for our home, but increased my income ten-fold, earned a free company car, our first family overseas trip, multiple accolades and became top 15 ranking in Australia and New Zealand within my company?

By creating balance between the masculine methods I'd been taught for years and the feminine ways I was instinctively drawn to. (I was yet to learn the specifics, my heart was telling me I was on the right track, though.) I found a way to combine the SMART goal, a masculine way of approaching a task with a HEART goal, the feminine flowing method.

It became my SMART HEART goal!

What's the difference between masculine and feminine and why do we need both?

Masculine tends to be linear with straight lines and jagged edges. It goes in one direction, it's slow to make progress and is bottom-line oriented. Masculinity rules the left side of the brain, logic, thought, risk and rush. It sees things in black and white with little grey in between. It takes things literally and rarely sways from the step-by-step process.

Feminine is fluid. It curves and flows. It's fast paced, moving in multiple directions at once. Femininity rules the right side of our brain, emotions, understanding, creativity and nurturing. The feminine creates, sees the big picture, the purpose and all the possibilities in between the steps.

How does this help with goal setting and accomplishments?

Women have up to 25% more connection between the left (masculine) and right (feminine) hemispheres of the brain, compared to men.

When we develop a goal with the bottom line in mind and the big picture, the steps and the process, the direction and the flow, what we create is a union between both parts of us.

A SMART goal offers us an opportunity to create logical, reasoned, linear steps to achieve success. It's Specific, Measurable, Attainable, Realistic and Timely. Great qualities to have, however it's missing something, isn't it?

It lacks feminine energy, movement and inspiration.

A HEART goal tugs at the heartstrings. It creates the big picture, the purpose if you like, of how the accomplishment will improve your life, influence the life of those around you and leave an impact as a result of the achievement.

HARMONIOUS – the accomplishment of the goal adds harmony to your life and more importantly, the doing of the goal creates harmony in your daily life experience.

EMOTIONAL – it stirs an emotion within you, deep in your gut, which inspires you when you think about the end result. It leaves you feeling happy, excited and content. The idea of not achieving it is bigger than any excuse you can come up with!

ALIGNMENT – with your Inspiration Motivator's list, with people who are most important to you in your life. If there is a conflict with the goal and any of these items, your motivation and inspiration will be conflicted. Be sure what you want aligns with what is most important to you.

REPRESENTS – and aligns with your power, passion and purpose. When you review how this outcome reflects with your Inspired Motivators (from the previous chapter), it both supports and enhances who you are and what you stand for.

TRUE – the result of achieving the goal continues to represent you and your truth.

A HEART goal gives meaning, substance, movement and femininity; it paints more detail into your end picture and ultimately will speak volumes to you when the BS tries to dominate and sabotage.

If we revisit the SMART goal of my kitchen, we can see that although it hit all the 'right' markers, it didn't keep me inspired.

When I combined it with HEART there was Harmony. Having a kitchen was definitely going to create the sense of peace my life was lacking.

It was Emotional. I knew if I failed we'd be stuck in dire straits a lot longer and the idea of being able to provide the kitchen for my family filled me with an immense pride.

I was Aligned. My family, their health and wellbeing were extremely important to me. My professional success was important to me. In order to achieve this goal, I had to develop professionally, which in turn supported my family with a kitchen!

It beautifully Represented my power (I was owning the BS of "I can't do it!" by proving to myself I could). My passions where enriched because as a result of working towards the goal, I was working with and helping many women, while helping myself and my family. It created more dimension to my purpose, to be an inspiration and positive influence to my family and the women in my team.

It was True! The only way I could achieve my desired outcome was by being me! I put my family first and used that as a drive to power my business.

After succeeding with the SMART HEART Goal combination, I used it as the basis of all my goals. It was rare for me to lose sight and motivation of my desires. In fact, to this date, every goal I've set myself, I've achieved. I honestly believe it is because of the SMART HEART formula!

CASE STUDY: Sidone – Married with 2 Children, Back to Study and Work after 9 Years at Home.

10 years ago, Sidone was diagnosed with depression. Constantly anxious and overwhelmed, she felt like a constant disappointment to family and friends. Sidone hated who and what she had become. With suicidal thoughts almost every day, she felt like a burden, like her family would be better off without her. "I am useless, worthless, a disappointment, ugly, disgusting, never good enough, lazy, selfish, unlovable. It would be better if I was not alive". This was the BS dominating Sidone's internal world.

The impact of this thinking stripped Sidone of her self-esteem to the point that she functioned in 'protection' mode. She performed tasks she knew she had to, yet found it difficult to show emotional love towards her children and husband. She often blamed them, which resulted in her resenting them, further adding to the internal BS battle within her. She dreamed of going back to university, developing her skills and finding satisfying employment. She didn't know what any of that looked like, nor did she believe she was capable of doing it.

Since working with me, Sidone now knows she doesn't need to be a perfect mother, wife, daughter or friend because she's a great woman as she is. "I no longer believe that my family would be better off without me. The anger and aggression I used to feel continuously has lessened dramatically – negativity creeps in every so often, but my confidence in overcoming it means its impact is minimal. I deal with the situations, one step at a time. I feel more comfortable in showing and receiving affection, love and intimacy with my family and the love of myself is growing. As of early 2017, I'm back at university with my sights set firmly on a new field for myself professionally!"

Now it's time for you to start exploring your first SMART HEART goal. Take the Inspired Motivators, your "this is important to me" knowledge from the previous chapter and put some oomph behind it so you can move past the BS stories that created the emotional fog and create direction and clarity for your life.

Have a think about one thing in your life you want to achieve. It could be a family goal, a holiday, a professional goal, or something personal for yourself.

If this is one of the first times you've considered a goal for yourself, I encourage you to take a deep breath. Even if you've done goal setting before, the following exercise is something you can do to let go of clutter and settle yourself.

Clear your mind. Find something to focus on, consciously become aware of what is all around you while keeping your eyes stationary on the point in front of you. Notice the noises. Take a deep breath and become aware of the space you've created. When in this space, ask yourself, "What is something I'd really like to achieve or create in my life?"

Write a few things down. Pick one causing the strongest emotional response and use it to create some SMART HEART traction.

Be SPECIFIC!

How can you MEASURE progress & success of this goal?

How is it ATTAINABLE? What do you need to do to ensure it is Attainable? What action steps do you need to take?

How is it REALISTIC?

Be TIMELY. When do you want it?

How does achieving this goal create HARMONY? When you think about working towards this goal, so the actual steps involved, does it add harmony to you? Or is there resistance? If there is resistance, what solutions can you identify now, so that you can avoid the resistance and remain in flow and harmony? Now, float out into the future, to a time when the goal has been achieved – how has the accomplishment added harmony to your life, and the life of those around you?

What EMOTIONS do you feel when you think about it? There are three answers with this one area. Firstly, have a think about how you would feel if you never achieved this goal? What feelings come to mind? You can use this negative 'what if' as motivation and action any time you feel flat!

If you were to imagine the ideal day where you are proactively working towards, and achieving action steps for this goal, how do you feel? How does it inspire or motivate you?

Now, float out into the moment when this goal has become your reality – how do you feel recognising that you've done it? List the emotions that bubble to the surface.

Tip: For any negative emotion that surfaces, either use the above 'expanded vision' strategy or the Red Flag/White Word exercise to neutralise the intensity and amplify the positive emotions that are stirred up

Does it ALIGN with what is most important to you? Can your Inspiration Motivators add depth to your goal because they are all in the same theme? How does it align with these things? Again, spend some time visualising how the goal and your Inspiration Motivators come together to support and add dimension to one another.

How does it REPRESENT your Power? In what ways does it represent your Passion? How does it highlight your Purpose? When your goal represents who you are, you will feel a strong conviction deep within you that what you want to achieve is right for you.

Is it TRUE? Will working towards and achieving this goal help you be the truest, most authentic version of you? In what ways?

Well done, you! Now you have a framework to work from! How does it feel, to have something to work towards, something to focus on, instead of trapping you in an emotionally foggy mess of BS? Something which sets you free, aligns with what is important to you, and provides you with clarity and direction for your life.

We aren't done yet! Oh, no! We are going to give you a major boost of confidence when it comes to your first SMART HEART goal. Are you ready? This involves you tapping into that beautiful, creative feminine part of you and using your brain to your absolute advantage.

Read through this exercise in its entirety first, then come back to work through it step by step. This enables you to stay in the flow.

When ready, close your eyes. Imagine you are standing in the day your SMART HEART goal has become your reality. Notice the outcome is even better than expected.

Visualise what you are doing, feel the accomplishment and success of your goal.

What are you doing? Are you sitting or standing? Are you still or moving? Be in that moment, see the world through the eyes of this future you, the you who has achieved your SMART HEART goal.

Who are you celebrating with?

What can you see as you look around?

What can you hear? What can you smell?

What are you saying to the people who are with you?

What are you saying to yourself, reflecting on how well it went and how good it is to have achieved your goal?

What are you feeling, as you absorb this moment in? Acknowledge all those positive feelings: pride, confidence, excitement and happiness.

Where in your body do you feel those things? How does it feel to experience pride? Confidence? Excitement, happiness and everything else you feel at that time?

Whatever the mind sees the body believes to be true. Turn up the volume of this moment. Turn up everything you see, so the colours are intense and electric with the energy of the accomplishment. Turn up the positive things you are saying to yourself. Turn up the positive feelings you feel. Allow yourself to be lost in the moment for as long as it feels right for you to do so.

This visualisation is the image you will assign to your SMART HEART goal. When you do the practical actions to make it real, use this visualisation to enthuse you. When you have a hit, use this visualisation to heal you. Revisit it regularly. Go to bed meditating on this visualisation. The more you visit it, the more your unconscious mind will search for evidence and opportunities to support it because this will be the track your mind pays attention to.

Tip Time

1. When setting a goal, think broadly. A goal can be anything you want to create in your life: personal improvement, professional improvement, relationship improvement, travelling and creating experiences. The list is limited only by your thinking.

2. Clear your mind before you start planning your goals. To do this:

    a. Lift your eyes above eye level and focus on something stationary in front of you.

    b. While continuing to look at this point, become aware of three things to the left of that point.

    c. Find three things to the right of that point. How far around can you see (while keeping your eyes still on that centre point?).

    d. Feel your head go calm. Feel the space. Ask yourself, "What is something I want to achieve in my life?" List them all on paper.

3. Pick one goal to work on for the moment. Make it a SMART HEART goal.

    a. Specific
    b. Measurable
    c. Attainable
    d. Realistic
    e. Timely
    f. Harmonious
    g. Emotional
    h. Aligned
    i. Representative of your power, passion and purpose
    j. True to you

4. Visualise the successful outcome of your goal.
    a. Where are you the day it becomes your reality?
    b. Who are you with?
    c. What do you see, hear and smell in that moment?
    d. What are you saying?
    e. What are you saying to yourself?
    f. What do you feel? Where do you feel it?
5. Use your SMART HEART goal and visualisation on a regular basis to keep you motivated and inspired.

Conclusion

The moment I claimed my power,
I was able to honour and live my passion.
The more I lived my passion, the clearer my purpose
became. This is my wish for you.

Bree Stedman

I'm sure you see the reason behind my passion for teaching women this information is because it is so valuable. It goes deeper than just 'try and be positive', doesn't it?

The thoughts in your head are real to you. Positive or negative, they have the ability to impact every waking moment. Owning your BS is not about squashing them down in the hopes they go away. It's not about ignoring them, or dishonouring yourself because you have a belief they are wrong. It's certainly not about revisiting the problem, trying to see it from as many different perspectives and views as you can. None of this is going to help, and *Owning your BS* is about helping you gain back what is rightfully yours: choice!

Owning your BS is ultimate power. It is being able to recognise that even though the stories are there, even though they have the potential to cause you pain, despair, overwhelm you and everything else, they are also there to teach. For you to use as a lesson to grow forward, towards the life you do want for yourself.

In the 5 years since I experienced my 'to-the-core transformation', my life has continued to have ups and downs. On more than one occasion, the BS blindsided me and took me away from flow. The knowledge I now have always helps me regain my power when I am ready to do so. For most of the time and space within me, my head talk and emotional centre of my body (my heart) is light, positive and carefree again.

I've done considerably more work than just apply these few conscious strategies to achieve the long-term change I have. However, the material I have shared in this book remains as my 'go to' when times are challenging. Both my kids, who at the time of writing this book, are 7 and 9, know how to use the power of their minds to move past challenging situations they struggle with. They, like all children, have their moments. As they are children, I still remind them regularly they do have a choice when it comes to the way they feel, as I need to remind myself at times as well! I know the gift I've given them with these strategies extends further than I can comprehend at this point in time.

Of a night time, when their heads are busy replaying events of the day, I hear them talking to themselves to create clarity. I hear them asking, "What can I do about it? Nothing right now, so take a deep breath, let it go and go to sleep." To which I often chuckle!

They correct Aaron and I. "Don't say *don't*, mum! You either will or you won't there's no such thing as try!" And my absolute favourite: "What are you going to do about it, mum?"

They know how to break down the stories in their heads, to manipulate the pictures to let go of the negative and create a more neutral, calming focus.

Alivia, in particular, has developed a beautiful habit of going straight to a strategy whenever she sees one of her friends upset. Instinctively, she knows it won't serve her friend to stay in the story of the event any longer than necessary, so I frequently see her use an adaptation of the expanded vision strategy I've shared with you with her friends. In fact she uses it on me, too!

They would not know this if it wasn't for me recognising I needed to address my own BS. I shudder when I think about the way our life would be now if that rock bottom moment didn't kick me in the bum and force me to change. I firmly believe we would not be as connected as we are now. I know I definitely wouldn't have the peace within me that I do.

Having read this book, chances are, you too are ready to regain your power. You've had enough of the BS affecting your life negatively. You are ready improve your own life and be a woman of influence to the people in your world – your family, children, friends and clients. Or maybe, just maybe as a result of this book, you already feel that you're on that journey, and that is exciting!

CASE STUDY: Katie - Engaged Mother of 4, Nursing Student

Katie's negative emotions ruled her life. Her guilt and forever trying to please everyone else ruled her head, home and heart. Seven weeks before her twin boys were born, she was put in hospital on bed rest. This physically limiting situation led the BS in her head to turn into a full blown party. With guilt from not being able to be with her older boys and guilt from feeling her body wasn't strong enough to bring the twins to term, the stories escalated to a point where 6 months post-partum, she hit her lowest point. Her mood swings, anger, anxiety, sadness and resentment all got the best of her and she started to have "I don't want to be here anymore", "I'm a horrible person", "My kids deserve a different mother" and "I'm not enough for them" thoughts.

The bottom line was that Katie hated the person she had become. She felt like the world was against her, nothing was going right and everything was in such a muddle. She felt she was not enough. The BS and emotional fog impacted every aspect of Katie's life. She never wanted to leave the house, and when she would she'd go straight back home. She had no patience with her kids, would frequently yell and shout and her house was full of anger. Every minute of every day she was angry, and as such the relationships with her fiancé and sons was cracking.

Then reality got real. Katie realised if she didn't get help, she would be creating another broken family, this time for her twins. She put the BS excuses to the side and took ownership. "My life is now such a happier place. My four kids are happy little souls. My partner and I are rebuilding our relationship, and I feel it is stronger than ever. I was able to recognise exactly how far I had come when a couple months after my breakthrough, my ex-husband filed a court motion for custody of my two older boys. During those three months, when I felt my world could literally fall apart at the seams, I used the strategies that Bree taught me and relied on my own inner strength to get through it. The head talk, just like my ex-husband, had no control over me or my emotions. Thankfully, we won the court case and as such my fiancé and I have been able to move to a town where I'm now able to complete my nursing degree, my older boys have settled into a great school, and we are busy rebuilding our lives with a strong sense of confidence, love and purpose. I'm able to co-parent with my ex-husband for my children's sake. I have a beautiful relationship with my children, I know what is important in my life and I am very excited for what my future holds for me and my family."

Throughout the course of this book I've shared with you the 3 Steps to Ultimate Ownership.

Power is the ability to recognise what no longer serves you and puts yourself into a position which enables you to create a shift, change or transformation.

I've introduced you to a lot of new information, concepts and strategies which are possibly out-of-the-box compared to other things you've learned in the past. Each strategy, suggestion and tool offers you the possibility to either create new choices, new ways of looking at things, or ways to create space from those events and thoughts not serving you.

Your power ultimately lies in your ability to stop telling the stories, stop getting caught up in BS and instead, approach your thoughts with a solution focus. The simplest way to do this is to ask any of the following 'what' questions:

- What am I thinking?
- What am I feeling?
- What can I do about it?
- What can I learn?
- What do I want to achieve?
- What is important to me in this moment?
- What is the purpose of this conversation/argument?
- What can I do differently?
- What can I do to help them/me/us?

These powerful questions give you the ability to see past the problem. If you feel the emotion still charging you in a way that doesn't serve you, remember the next thing you can do to own that BS is expand what you are focusing on, become aware of more than the problem and physically notice all you can see and hear around you.

Lastly, your power, your real power, comes from living your life according to your Female Factor. Embrace your beautiful female brain and that cycle of yours. At times when you are in a slump, use it to restore and nurture yourself.

Plan your most dynamic activity around the time when your hormones, mental clarity and physical energies are at their highest – they are there to support you! Likewise for your connection and creativity phases. Each phase has its strengths and weakness, and when you can work out what they mean for you, you create a cyclic plan for success and happiness.

The absolute most important of all of 'what' I've taught, however, is the recognition that you and only you must make a choice to create the change. As mentioned in Chapter 2, for as long as you blame other people and external situations for your current position in life, you will continue to feel powerless to change. The moment you stand up and say "ENOUGH! I'm ready to own it now!" is the moment your power returns to you. From that point forward, anything becomes possible.

To live a life with passion is to live a life of your design. Passion is the fuel of life; it gives you an opportunity to experience zest and to create memories that warm your heart and fulfil your soul.

Own Your BS has given you a good nudge toward identifying what makes your heart sing, and if you've followed the suggestions and created a plan to support your Inspiration Motivators, those things which are most important to you, chances are you are feeling passion emerge as a sensational part of your life. Give yourself time to explore what is important to you on a regular basis. As with life, they change and grow as you continue to transform.

My heartfelt encouragement to you is continue to make choices which support the things you identified as your Inspiration Motivators. It's not always going to be possible. When it is, if you make your decisions based on how it will support what is most important to you, I'm confident you will not only notice the amount of BS that clears from your life, but plenty of examples that leave you feeling grateful, satisfied and content. Your passion for life can be as simple as choosing to live in alignment with what's important to you, and avoiding anything that conflicts with those things.

Hannah was a beautiful young girl I worked with years ago and she follows this philosophy religiously. When asked how it's changed her life, she told me, "Bree, it's like this – if it feels right, I do it. If it doesn't, I don't. The more I follow this rule, the more I notice my life as being easy – more than easy, amazing. I now have a job that I absolutely adore, a partner who respects and cherishes me, and strong, connected relationships with the people who are most important to me. And I believe that's all been possible because I come back to my list of values – if it's going to take me away from that list, I don't do it."

Sounds simple, right? Remember it's only as complicated as you allow it to be, so focus on this instead of doubting it. Ask yourself:

"What would happen in my life if I chose to do things supporting my list of Inspiration Motivators?"

Purpose. What is the ultimate reward from owning your BS? It's knowing what your purpose for today is.

Being able to wake up every day knowing that no matter what happens, you have the power within you to redirect how your day progresses.

It's having the awareness of what is most important to you, the fuel motivating you to live your day with passion.

It's the acknowledgement that although you can't change the past and you can't predict the future, you can control how you respond and what you create now.

It's the confidence, direction and clarity that comes from being able to influence your own life experience and the lives of those around you.

At the end of the day, that is the purpose of this book. I shared my journey and my wisdom with you in the hope you are able to identify that although the BS can be painful, it's there as a lesson for you. It's there for you to use as ammunition to be the absolute best version of you that you can be. It's there for you to grow, to lead by example and to show the world BS does not need to consume you.

Go. Experience all life is going to throw at you. The ups, downs, challenges and accomplishments. Be a master at learning through your experiences. Enjoy each adventure that comes your way. Always remember, when the emotional fog clouds over, you can transform your circumstances by asking:

"Am I ready to own this BS?"

Acknowledgements

The journey that lead to this book would not have been possible without the love, support and encouragement from the following people. Writing this I recognise how incredibly blessed I am, as there are so many people that I could mention. Thank you to all of the people in my life, past, present and future for the friendship, support and love you give me.

To my husband, Aaron. You are my rock. You came into my life at a time when I had such little love and belief for myself. You built me up, and then you gave me the space to grow into the woman I am today. All the while by loving me for who I am. The life we've built together has been richer than I'd ever imagined and I can't wait to see where we go to from here. I love you.

To my children, Blair and Alivia. The journey of being your mum has been more than I ever imagined. Words will never fully explain the impact that you have on my life – you are my inspiration, my grace-growers, my drive and purpose. Thank you for being the spirited, unique and perfectly amazing little people that you are.

Mum. Without a doubt, you are one of the strongest women I know. You have always been behind me – you are my soundboard, my shoulder and my support. Thank you so very much for believing in me when I questioned myself. I can't tell you how much I love that you too are living your life on your terms, with complete Emotional Confidence now. You are the epitome of dignity and self respect.

Dad, you encouraged me from a young age to follow my heart and strengths. To live life by following my passions and making choices that fulfil life. You've always supported my choices to build businesses outside of 'the square'. You inspire me because you have always lived your life to the fullest. This has been such a beautiful thing to both watch and learn from.

To all the coaches and mentors who have influenced me and encouraged me to grow. Your wealth of knowledge has completely transformed my life – you all amaze me with your commitment to your missions – the world is a better place because of the courage and determination you consistently live by. Thank you for your wisdom and guidance.

To my extended family, friends and clients. I feel so lucky that my life is full of so many of you! You have supported me during all the phases of my life. I cherish the memories that we've created and the journey that we share. You ground me and you inspire me. I'm so grateful to you all.

www.ingramcontent.com/pod-product-compliance
Ingram Content Group UK Ltd.
Pitfield, Milton Keynes, MK11 3LW, UK
UKHW020140250726
13967UKWH00002B/770